Practical
Sail Care and Repair

Lisa Carr

Published by Waterline Books
an imprint of Airlife Publishing Ltd
101 Longden Rd, Shrewsbury, England.

ISBN 1 85310 463 9

A Sheerstrake production.

A CIP catalogue record of this book
is available from the British Library.

All Photographs and illustrations by Lisa Carr.

This is a book for all those of you who have the courage to pursue your dream – from a sailmaker who knows the problems of fixing sails at sea.

With special thanks to John McKillop who taught me so much, and to George Taylor who encouraged me (more than he'll ever know) just when I needed it most.

Contents

Introduction

Most books and articles on the care and repair of sails have been written by sailmakers in the comfort and space of a sail loft. It is another thing entirely to be at sea in a Force Eight gale with the last headsail blown out, and at least a couple of days to go before landfall, with, even then, the prospect of finding a reliable sailmaker doubtful.

The cruising yachtsman can do much to prevent seventy-five percent of the damage that happens to sails, but despite all care being taken, there is still that extra strong gust of wind, that batten caught in the shroud, that un-noticed bit of chafe that could catch you unawares and far from land with a useless sail.

So I would like to offer some suggestions on the danger points to look out for and how to strengthen them, and later on how to make emergency repairs at sea that could hold your sails together long enough to get the boat safely into harbour. Then we can look at ways to turn your instant repairs into a permanent and more professional job.

I have also added a few ideas for items that you can make, designed for space saving, money saving – and possibly life-saving!

Sails: A Reference Guide

Sails should be built to suit your boat and *your* purpose. Racing sails for instance, are designed for the maximum sail area which will conform to the rules, but not for a long life. Cruising sails however, should be built to last with an eye to maximum strength and minimum maintenance.

It is important to find a sailmaker who will listen, help and advise you. For example, some sail lofts are not prepared to make a battenless mainsail; some will offer you a 'computer designed' sail that may not suit your long-term needs, so it is worth looking and asking around to find a sailmaker who will listen to your ideas and explain what is wrong with them from his professional viewpoint – but who will also be prepared to compromise if he feels that you know what you are talking about.

There are many excellent books available on the different kinds of rig, the latest sail designs, the latest sail materials – but since this book is primarily for the 'practical' and 'cruising' sailor, the following diagrams may be of help, particularly to those who are new to sailing.

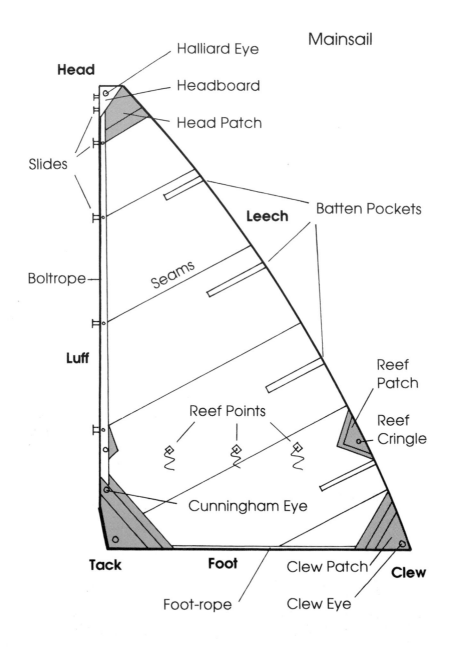

Mainsail

Halliard Eye

Head

Headboard

Head Patch

Slides

Leech

Batten Pockets

Boltrope

Seams

Luff

Reef Patch

Reef Points

Reef Cringle

Cunningham Eye

Tack

Foot

Clew Patch

Clew

Foot-rope

Clew Eye

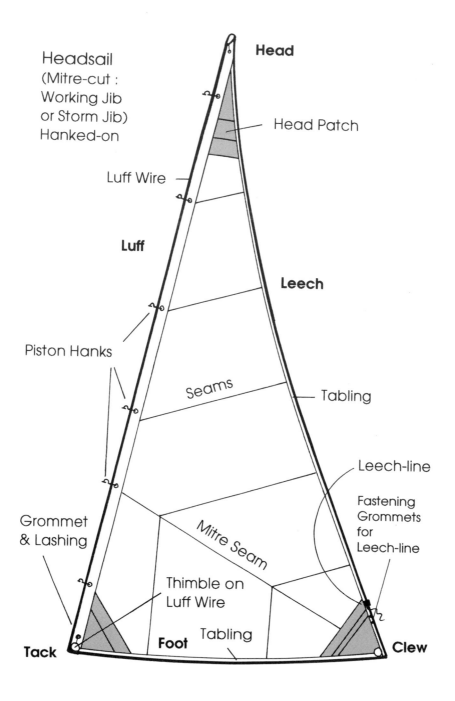

Headsail
(Mitre-cut :
Working Jib
or Storm Jib)
Hanked-on

Head

Head Patch

Luff Wire

Luff

Leech

Piston Hanks

Seams

Tabling

Leech-line

Fastening
Grommets
for
Leech-line

Grommet
& Lashing

Mitre Seam

Thimble on
Luff Wire

Foot

Tabling

Tack

Clew

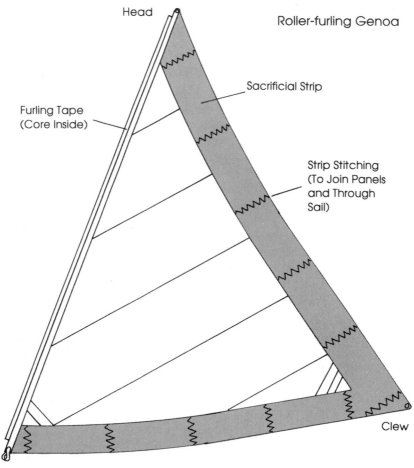

Head

Roller-furling Genoa

Sacrificial Strip

Furling Tape
(Core Inside)

Strip Stitching
(To Join Panels
and Through
Sail)

Clew

Tack
(Webbing to Shackle to Lower Drum)

Tips on Sail Care

Cleanliness

Hose down sails whenever possible to remove salt and airborne sand or grit. Before packing them away for the winter, soak them overnight in fresh water with a little washing-up liquid added. If necessary scrub stubborn stains with a soft brush taking care not to damage the stitching. Make sure that the sails are completely dry before stowing them away.

Stowage

Headsails

Pack as loosely as possible into bags which are large enough and of a suitable material to allow the sail to 'breathe'.

Main or Mizzen

Shake out any reefs, flake the sail onto the boom and secure it with ties; and most important *put on that sail cover!* This should ideally be made of one hundred percent Acrylic (YachtCrillic™ TempoTest™ etc.) which is water resistant and UV proof. Canvas, though cheaper, will soak up rain and deteriorate in the sun, while PVC or plastic, though practical for a quick 'wipe-off', encourages condensation which will over a period of a few months cause mold spots to form on the sailcloth.

Stowing Sails

Sails that are in constant use are better off loosely bagged, as they will not be constantly creased along the same lines. If however, you plan to store them over the winter or have limited stowage space on your boat, they should be folded. (Preferably when clean and dry and on a slightly different fold line every time.)

There are different methods of folding sails according to which sail and where you are doing it.

The professional way is called 'Flaking'; folding the sail in a concertina, roughly parallel to the foot. This requires two people and a large clean space on which to spread the sail.

The 'single-handed' fold and the 'on-board' stow are more practical aboard most cruising yachts

Try to avoid flaking a sail along the same folds every time as this can weaken the cloth over a period of time.

Although I have only illustrated a mainsail, the following methods can also be used on jibs, genoas, cruising chutes or spinnakers. (For the latter, use the 'single-handed' fold; bring both clews together and fold the centre foot to them.)

Properly folded, you will be surprised at how little space a seemingly bulky sail will occupy.

Fig 1 Flaking a Mainsail →
This is the professional's way and requires two people and a smooth surface on which to lay the sail out.
The folds should be approximately two thirds the width of the sail bag and at right angles to the ieech. (To avoid distorting the battens.)
Try also to avoid folds in the head, tack and clew patches.

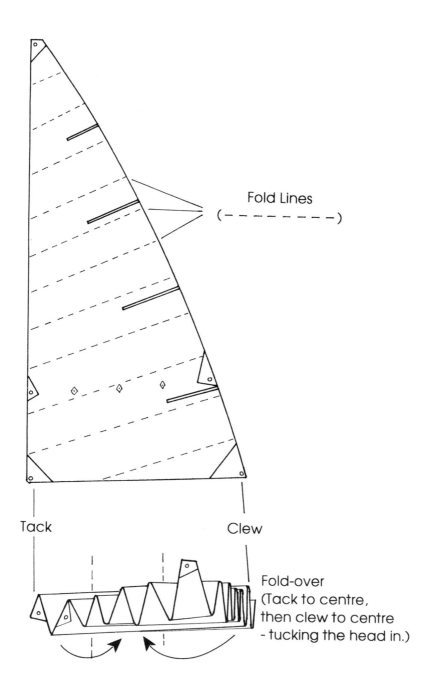

Fold Lines
(– – – – – – – – –)

Tack

Clew

Fold-over
(Tack to centre,
then clew to centre
- tucking the head in.)

Fig 2 Mainsail – The Single-handed Fold→
The advantage of this method is that even if you
have to fold your sail on a rough (eg.concrete)
surface, there is no need to drag it over the ground
which may damage the cloth or snag the stitching.

The distance between the vertical fold lines will
depend mainly on the length of the longest batten
and the height of the sail bag. It may be more
practical, in terms of stowage space, to have three
folds rather than two, which will make the rolled-up
sail shorter but bulkier.

Tie off the head of the sail to a bollard on the
quay or weight it down with something heavy
enough to allow you to pull against it. Pick up the
tack and fold it towards the clew, brushing any
loose sand or grit from the exposed area. Holding
the first fold, lay the two layers over the last third
and brush it off. Fold the sail in half, head to clew,
then roll it loosely from the fold downwards,
cleaning it as you go. It can then be bagged and
stowed.

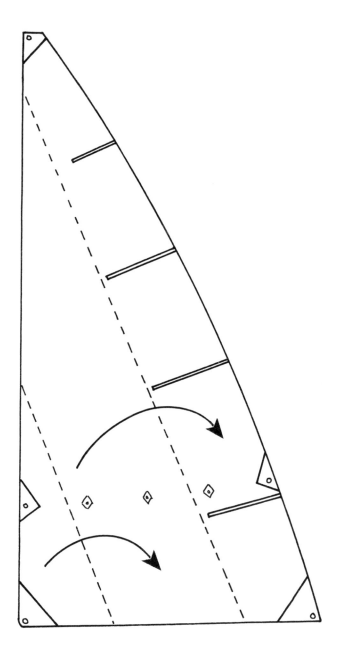

First Fold   Second Fold

Bagging a sail on board can be difficult due to lack of space. With a hanked-on headsail it is possible to flake it along the side-deck while it is still attached to the forestay, using hanks to form the folds. Remove the sheets, stretch the foot so that it lies flat and flake the leech down over it. Fold the clew one third over towards the tack and roll forwards from this fold to the forestay. When you have almost reached the tack, unclip the hanks and roll the sail over the luff. This will give you a fairly compact bundle , though not as neat as if it were done ashore.

If the headsail has a wire luff, care should be taken to avoid kinking it. Ideally the luff should be rolled and the coil laid flat onto the sail which should then be rolled round it. If this is not possible, use the previous method; but rather than rolling the clew forward, fold it approximately every metre, stopping three metres from the tack. Un-hank the sail from the forestay and lay the wire luff in loose loops in a figure of eight pattern over the body of the sail, which should then be folded over it from side to side.

To fold a mainsail on board, the simplest way is to take it off, reverse it (tack to clew-point) and lay it over the boom. Then flake it down onto the cabin top which will make it easier to line up the leech and avoid twisting the battens.

Chapter 1
Sails and Cruising

Most blue-water cruising folk are sailing on a budget. Half the ones that I have met are either young people who have worked and saved for a year – or several – to enable them to cruise as long as the money holds out. Others are older people who, with their children fully grown and departed home, have decided that there is nothing to keep them back any longer or retired people who are finally realising the way of life that they have dreamed of for years.

Besides these, there are the rest of us – the unclassifiable ones who follow this lifestyle because we cannot imagine any other way of living. And we are, all of us, probably the last of the truly free people.

Free, however, as long as the money holds out and the wind still blows. On a cruising yacht the main expenses (after food) have to be on the motive powers – sails and engine.

When you are cruising, perhaps day-hopping in the Mediterranean or Caribbean, or ocean crossing, unless you have an unlimited supply of fuel and a powerful engine, it is the sails that will eventually get the boat to her destination. But even though they may have been built by the finest sailmaker in the world, they are still a yacht's workhorse and subjected to severe abuse.

Your sails will last far longer if they are treated with care and attention.

Try to avoid over-stressing or stretching the fabric by carrying too light a sail (or too much sail) for the prevailing wind conditions. It is better to shorten sail by reefing or changing down ahead of time rather than five minutes too late. (Those few minutes can do a lot of damage which may not be apparent until later – too late!)

When raising a sail, watch carefully that it will hoist clear of any obstacles; this applies particularly to the mainsail where the headboard and battens can catch on or under the spreaders or into the shrouds. (Seventy-five percent of repairs to mainsails are due to the dreaded disease called BATT POX.)

When using a hanked headsail, make sure that the hanks can run freely up the forestay and that there are no twists in the luff.

If you have roller-furling headsails, it is important to ensure that the extrusions are exactly aligned and that there are no rough corners at the joins that will cause wear on the luff tape.

When dropping a sail, if you have to pull on it, haul down on the luff (rather than the leech) as it is far stronger and will not cause the sailcloth to stretch. If you have roller-reefing round the boom, take up hard on the topping lift before releasing the main halyard (to avoid excessive strain on the leech) and if possible fit a disc of six millimetres aluminium (with well smoothed edges) at the gooseneck to stop the luff-rope riding forward and possibly jamming. If you have to reef above the second batten, it is an idea to pad the inner end of the batten with an old towel or piece of foam to stop it pressing onto and distorting the sailcloth. It will also help to prevent the batten twisting (which can happen if the sail is wound too tightly round the boom).

If you are motorsailing, (as is so often the case in the Mediterranean where there is either no wind or too much right on the nose), drop the headsail – unless you have a flat-cut jib or Yankee. Also tighten down on the main, either using the Cunningham, flattening reef or lower reef; a flat sail can help your speed by a knot or two and steady the boat, but unless it is tied over with a preventer it will flog back and forth, damaging itself and your nerves!

If you are lying at anchor in a harbour where a swell or surge can cause the boat to roll, making life uncomfortable on board, a reefed mizzen (on a ketch) or a double reefed main (on a sloop), can help ease the motion if sheeted down as flat and hard as possible. A storm trysail (if you have one) could be used instead of the mainsail; but a more effective method is to hoist your storm jib (hanked onto the backstay, tack uppermost) using the main halyard. The will provide the maximum area at the highest and most effective point; a single sheet should be led to a halyard winch on the mast so that the sail can be tightened until it is completely flat. (If this is the only time you ever have to use your storm jib – you are lucky!)

There are, however, other uses for this small but versatile sail. In very light airs it can be come a 'water sail' to fill the slot below the boom – this is an old trick used by the Breton gaff-rigged fishing boats – and it works! The head attaches to the gooseneck, with the luff running below the boom; the tack ties off at the boom end, (or as far out as possible) and a light line from the clew fastens to the lower block on the mainsheet. This makes it an extension of the mainsail and self-tacking. (Although it could be in the way in the cockpit on a modern sloop – , it is worth a try.)

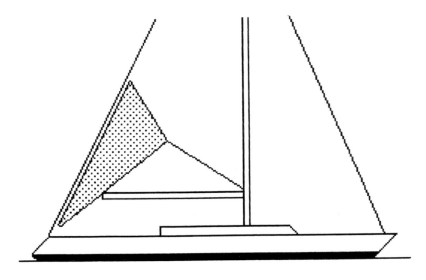

Storm jib used as a steadying sail.

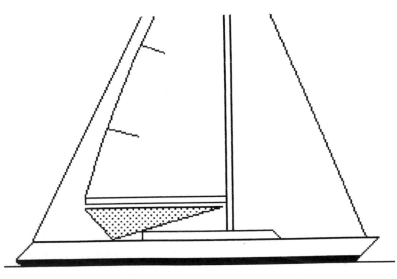

Storm jib used as a 'water sail'.

Fig 3

Sail Cleaning

When you arrive in a port after days at sea, don't you feel better after a fresh-water shower? Well, so will your sails!

Cleaning, washing and covering sails will not only improve their appearance , but also prolong their working life.

Airborne sand, grit and salt will collect in the seams and abrade the cloth and stitching, so hose sails with fresh water whenever possible. Alternatively, take advantage of rain showers to do the job for you, as long as the wind is not too strong and you can be sure to dry the sails afterwards.

Before packing a sail away for any length of time, check it over for damage and try to remove any stains; after treatment the sail should be soaked overnight in warm water with liquid detergent and then rinsed thoroughly. Make sure it is completely dry before stowing it. (See 'Tips on Sail Care')

Stain Removal

The most likely stains to appear on a sail (most of which you can prevent from reappearing if you can find what caused them) are rust, mildew, oil, tar, grease, adhesives – and messages from the seagull who has taken up residence on your spreaders or masthead!

Some of the cleaning methods mentioned use toxic, damaging or flammable chemicals, so all care should be taken while trying them. Wear rubber gloves, avoid splashing (keep a bucket of fresh water to hand and wear old clothes), do not smoke and work out of doors whenever possible (or in a well ventilated situation). If in doubt, try the method on a small piece of sailcloth first, preferably one with a similar stain.

Stains – Possible Causes & Cures

Rust – Causes

Luff wire, swage at the head or tack (even stainless wire can mark cloth and if galvanised wire is used, this is liable to break at the swage allowing water to seep in and rust the broken end).

Sail stowed near rusting paint or food tins.

Headsail when dropped at anchor allowed to rest on the anchor chain.

Wire strands from a rotary brush. If used on a drill these can break off and fly some distance – easily caught in a sail and remain unnoticed until the damp causes rust to start.

Sail Covers; if fastened with turn-buttons which my be riveted on with ferrous rivets. If grommets and lashing are used, grommets may rust unless brass or stainless steel ones are used. In either case, they should be removed and patched if necessary before installing non-ferrous ones.

Rust – Prevention

Check luff wires and swaged eyes.

Cover sails. Put headsails into bags – if leaving them hanked on, tie the bag to the top lifeline.

Main/Mizzen should be protected by a fitted (not too tight) cover fastened around the mast and under the boom.

Rust – Cure

There are many 'Rust Removers' on the market, but read the directions first since many are not suitable for textiles. (It is better to have a sound but stained sail, rather than a pristine one with weak patches.)

Chemical Remedies

Oxalic Acid (poisonous)
Can be bought as crystals from most chemists.

1oz dissolved in half a litre of water in a plastic or glass dish – NOT metal.

Soak stained area for one to two hours then rinse well.

Hydrochloric Acid
Two percent as above.

Organic Remedies
Rhubarb!
This contains oxalic acid and is cheap when in season. Cook with a little water until mushy, spread the paste onto rust spots and leave for one to two hours before rinsing off. (I have not tried this myself but I am told that it works.)

Mildew – Causes
Sails packed while damp and salt not washed out. (Salt crystals will attract moisture.)

Sails stored in a damp and badly ventilated place.

Sail cover made of PVC or other type of non-breathing material.

Mildew – Prevention
Wash the salt out of the sail and dry it thoroughly before stowing.

Mildew – Cure
To remove marks, soak them in warm water and biological detergent overnight. Scrub gently with a soft brush or soak the stained patches in the same mixture with a little bleach if they do not respond to the previous treatment.

Rinse well afterwards.

Oil, Tar, Grease and Diesel – Causes
Unnoticed spillage of engine oil.

Diesel leakage into bilges.

Tar on shoes transferred to the deck after a trip ashore.

Fuel on deck after topping up.

Handling a sail after working on the engine.

Hoisting a sail after the application of sun tan lotion to hands and body.

Anchor hoisted through oil or tar pollution and leaving a residue on the foredeck.

Oil, Tar, Grease and Diesel – Prevention

Keep a pair of 'shore-going' shoes and keep your 'deck' shoes for wear aboard.

Take any headsails onto the foredeck through the fore-hatch whenever possible, rather than dragging them through the cockpit.

Wash the deck with a detergent after refuelling.

Oil, Tar, Grease and Diesel – Cure

If the stain is recent wash in biological detergent and warm water as soon as possible.

If the stain is well set in, soak in Acetone for fifteen minutes. This should dissolve it sufficiently (without damaging the sailcloth).

Rub it over gently with a sponge moistened with 'Jif™' or any non-scratch cleaner but remember to avoid the stitching. This should remove almost all the marks.

Remember to rinse the sail well in fresh water.

Adhesives – Causes

Sail insignia or numbers if they peel off can leave an unsightly residue.

Also patches that have been glued as emergency repairs with contact cement.

Adhesives – Prevention

If your sail has numbers or other motifs on it, it is worthwhile stitching them in place if the corners or edges start to lift.

If you have to make an emergency patch, use clear contact adhesive (UHU™, Clear Bostick™ etc) rather then the cheaper brown coloured variety.

Adhesives – Cure

To remove old adhesive, rub it from the edges inward with a clean, dry cloth to remove the loose bits. Then rub with a petroleum derivative such as naphtha or carbon tetrachloride (available from some chemists or dry-cleaners).

Blood Stains – Causes

Accidental cuts, scratches etc. Possibly mutiny!

Blood Stains – Cure

If possible soak the stain in cold fresh water. (If the stain is more than a few hours old, salt water will only set it in more firmly.)

If it is a fresh bloodstain try a dressmaker's remedy; find a clean piece of cloth and chew it until it is saturated with saliva and rub it over the stain until the mark has almost gone, then soak it in fresh water, rinsing frequently until no trace of the colour remains.

Seagulls – Prevention

Seagull droppings can stain your sails and covers, so it pays to discourage them. To prevent them perching on the masthead hoist an old flag, a fish kite or anything else that is light enough to flutter in the lightest wind. At the spreaders, tie a couple of strips of spinnaker nylon onto the flag halyards and hoist them as high as possible. Anything fluttering up there will make these aviators think twice about landing.

Seagulls – Cure

Remove the dried remains and soak the cover, sail or whatever in warm, slightly salty water with some biological detergent added – preferably overnight. If necessary scrub the marks gently. Rinse very well and dry thoroughly.

As long as the bird has been eating a normal seagull diet, this should shift any marks!

Sail Protection

A sail's worst enemy is the sun. As a rough guide, every month that they are left exposed to the UV rays will take a year off their life. Therefore sail cover and sailbags are a necessity; but if yours happen to fall to bits or takes to the ocean and you cannot find a sailmaker, why not try your hand at making them yourself?

Sail Covers

To make a sail cover you need a few basic measurements. You will also need a sewing machine, zigzag stitch and/or straight-stitch (or endless patience) and the following items:

Sewing shears
An office-size stapler
Tape measure
Tailor's chalk
Graph paper
Sail cover hooks and eyes (or hooks and grommets).
3mm cord (braided leech-line is ideal).
Two short lengths of Velcro™.
Double-sided tape.

First, stow the sail on the boom as you would normally, not too neat a stow or your cover will end up being too tight. Then, following Figure 4, fill in the measurements.

a) Height from top of sail to underside of boom.

b) Measurement around the mast. (Including halyards if you wish to leave them on.)

c) Length of boom from centre front of mast to end of sail.

d) Measurement around the boom. (Make sure that there is 5cm of boom from the end of the sail to enable the collar to sit neatly).

e) Measure 50cm back from the centre of the mast and then measure around the sail and under the boom; divide this measurement in half.

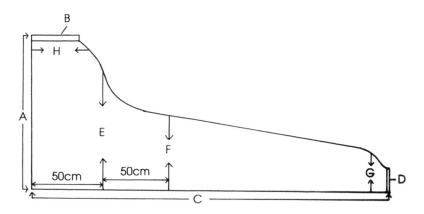

Fig 4

f) Measure back another 50cm and do the same.

g) At the clew of the sail do the same.

h) At the head of the sail, where the headboard sticks out, do the same. This measurement should be on the loose side otherwise the headboard can wear through the cover.

Take a piece of graph paper and draw Figure 4 to scale, adding 3cm to the bottom of the hem and 5cm to the front hem and reducing the collars to 1cm. Your drawing should then look like the wrong side in Fig 5. Now you need to know what type of material and how much of it you will need.

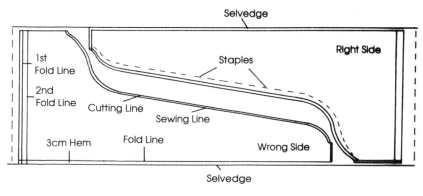

Fig 5

The best material to use is acrylic, sold under various trade names of which Yachtcrillic, Sunbrella and Tempotest are probably the best known and easily available. It is a man-made fabric, guaranteed UV resistant for five years, washable and water resistant; but it breathes, unlike PVC which when used for a cover can cause condensation and therefore encourage mould spots on the sail. Acrylic comes in various widths – choose the widest available for fewer joins.

Make two cut-outs of your drawing, draw to the same scale the width of your material and lay the cut-outs on it as in Figure 5. (If measurement 'A' is greater than the width, as in Figure 6.) Then measure the total length required (not forgetting that in Figure 6 you will have to get extra for the added-on parts), convert it back to metres and go buy your material.

In the same way that you did it on the graph paper, make the first drawing onto the cloth with tailor's chalk. This can easily be erased if you make a mistake. Mark the sewing line and allow 1cm seam allowance outside this – this is the cutting line. Cut along this line, pick up the piece and turn it so that the selvedge matches the opposite side (See Figure 5). Then staple the two pieces together, far enough inside the sewing line for the machine foot to avoid the staples.

If measurement 'A' is greater than the width of the cloth it will be necessary to add the extra piece (See Figure 6) to both sides before cutting and stapling. When you have added the piece to the first side, cut and reverse it. You will now see where the extra material is required to be added on the second side.

If your stapler will not reach far enough inside the stitching line, trim off excess material to match the first side. You will then be left with a long strip, slightly on the bias. Reserve this for the mast and boom collars. (See Figure7)

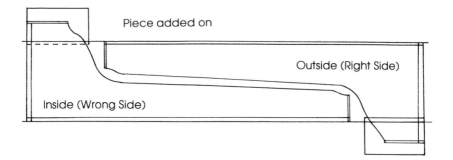

Piece added on

Outside (Right Side)

Inside (Wrong Side)

Fig 6

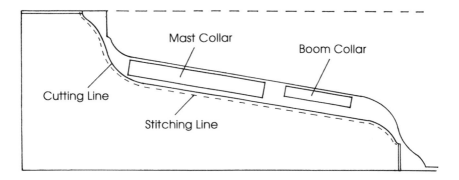

Mast Collar

Boom Collar

Cutting Line

Stitching Line

Fig 7

Turn the sewing machine to straight-stitch and sew down the stitching line. If you have a hot-knife (or soldering iron) run it down the line of the cutting edge to seal it, making cuts towards the stitching line at the inward curves. Remove the staples. Now, starting from the narrowest end, spread the cover open, right side up, and stitch (preferably with a wide zigzag) down just to the right of the seam, over the seam allowance. This makes for a neater finish and although the exposed thread will perish faster, the first line of straight stitching will hold the cover together as it is not exposed to the sunlight.

Then turn under the 3cm hem along the bottom selvedges and sew it down with two rows of stitching. For the front, turn under 1cm and under again by 4cm and stitch twice. (These hems can be pressed down with a warm iron or stapled to keep them in place for sewing.)

For the mast collar, take measurement 'B' and add 12cm to the length. Cut a strip this length and 15cm wide, sealing one long edge with a hot-knife. Place the other edge against the edge of the cover where it goes round the mast, right sides together, pulling the body of the cover straight to match the collar. Sew along the stitching line (See Figure 8). Turn the collar up, pressing the seam allowance towards it. Then fold it back on itself and stitch the ends (See Figure 9). Now turn it right side out and, matching the sealed edge of the first line of stitching, crease the top edge with your finger and staple (or iron) it to hold it in place while you sew round the collar.

Cut a piece of Velcro the length of the overlap and sew one part to the overlap on the wrong side and the other part to the collar on the right side. Take a length of 3mm cord two and a half times the measurement of 'B' and stitch it to the centre of the collar. (See Figure 10) For the boom collar, follow the same method, but make the width 9cm instead of 15cm.

An alternative method of fastening the cover round the mast and boom is to add 7cm to the top and end of your cut-out material (instead of 1cm for the seam allowance). This should, for the mast, be parallel to the selvedge; and for the boom at right angles to it. (A collar round the mast looks neater, however, and is as easy to fasten.)

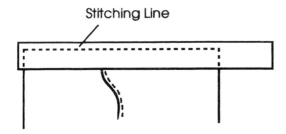

Stitching Line

Fig 8

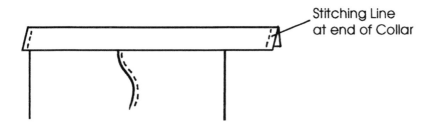

Stitching Line
at end of Collar

Fig 9

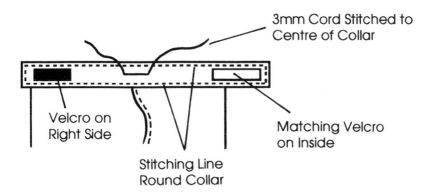

3mm Cord Stitched to
Centre of Collar

Velcro on
Right Side

Matching Velcro
on Inside

Stitching Line
Round Collar

Fig 10

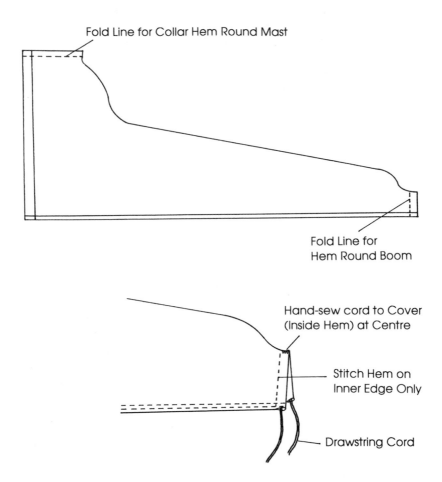

Fold Line for Collar Hem Round Mast

Fold Line for
Hem Round Boom

Hand-sew cord to Cover
(Inside Hem) at Centre

Stitch Hem on
Inner Edge Only

Drawstring Cord

Fig 11

When you have stitched the hems on the front
and bottom (See Figure 11), turn in 1 cm at the top
and end, and then in 3cm and sew along the inner
edge only. Thread the correct length of cord (2½
times the measurement) through the hem,
matching the ends, and catch the cord with needle
and thread at the seam line to prevent it pulling
out. This will give you a 'drawstring' effect.

Now you have to decide how you want to fasten the cover. There are several alternatives. The easiest method (and probably the most durable) is to use sew-on hooks and eyes made of nylon; your sailmaker should be able to supply you with these. A normal sewing machine should be able to stitch through the flat plate of nylon to attach them to the cover. You will need to sew back and forth a couple of times on each one. On the front they need to be about 30cm apart and on the bottom about 75cm – 100cm apart, starting from 20cm aft the mast.

Some people prefer to use sew-on hooks on one side of the cover with pairs of grommets on the other and a length of cord or shock-cord threaded through. The disadvantage of shockcord is that it will eventually lose its elasticity when exposed to long periods of sunlight. Another method is matched eyelets on both sides of the cover and a single lacing through, but this is time consuming to fasten, as are sewn on ties. It is also possible to use 'turnbuttons' but I would not recommend these since the backing plate has sharp edges which will easily cut through the fabric and pull out. Anyway, any metal snaps will eventually corrode and need replacing – however, the choice is yours.

Your cover is now ready for fitting. If you have winches or a mast ladder on that part of the mast that must be covered, then provision must be made to allow for them either by cutting holes or adding extruded covers.

For a mast ladder, the rungs of which are best left exposed, measure the height and width of the step and cut a rectangle of cloth 10cm longer and wider. Then mark on it the exact size of the step, in the centre and on the wrong side of the fabric patch. Then seal the edges of the patch with a hot-knife. Mark the outline of the step onto the cover and place the patch onto this, right sides together and matching the outline of the step. Cut the centre (See Figure 12) then turn the facing to the inside

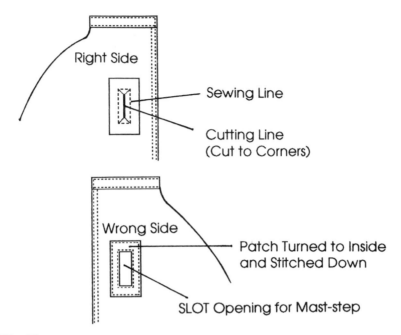

Fig 12

and stitch it down twice around – once close to the hole and then around the edge of the facing.

Follow the same procedure for winches using a circle instead of a rectangle if you wish to leave them exposed. However, if you want to keep them under the cover and the sail-cover is not loose enough to fit comfortably over them, you will have to add an extrusion.

Firstly mark the exact centre of the winch on the sail-cover.

Then for your extruded winch cover, measure round the base and measure the height of the winch and cut a rectangle of material to this size, plus 2cm for seam allowance. Use π^2 to find the radius of the circle or if you are not mathematically minded measure around a plate, bowl etc. of nearly the same circumference. Then cut a circle of cloth and stitch it to the side piece before you sew up the short side.

Photo 1. This sail cover extends over all the mast fittings comfortably, but you may wish to allow mast steps to protrude or make additional provision for mast winches.

By using this technique, you can present it to the winch to make sure it is not too small. It should not fit too tightly because the sail cover itself will hold it in place and it will need to be a little manoeuvrable. When you have ascertained that the fit is satisfactory (and this should be done with the fabric inside out), match the short edges together, mark the sewing line and then stitch along it. Turn the cover right side out and check again that the fit is satisfactory.

Mark a circle on the sail-cover, using a compass or the like, to position the cover. Draw another circle 1cm inside the first to provide your cutting line. Notch the seam allowance to just inside the first circle that becomes the stitching line. (See Figure 13)

Run a band of double-sided tape around the right side of the winch cover base to hold it in place for sewing. On the inside, mark a line on the base 1cm up from the raw edge as a sewing guide-line. To fit the cover for stitching it will be more convenient if you fill it with paper to give it its correct shape. Now peel off the protective paper from the double-sided tape and push the cover through the hole from the right side until line A meets line B. (See Figure 14).

Press the notched seam allowance against the double-sided tape, turn the sail-cover over and carefully straight-stitch along the line inside the winch cover. Press the seam allowance up into the winch cover and zigzag stitch it from the outside. (See Figure 15)

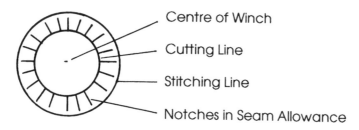

Centre of Winch

Cutting Line

Stitching Line

Notches in Seam Allowance

Fig 13

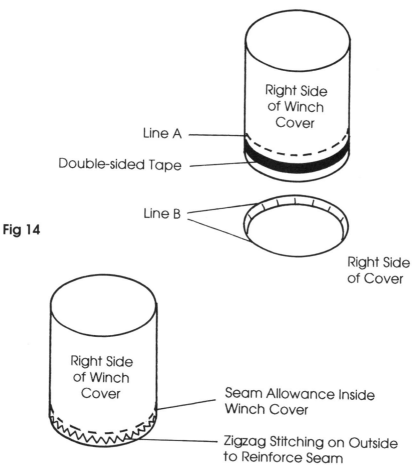

Right Side of Winch Cover

Line A

Double-sided Tape

Line B

Fig 14

Right Side of Cover

Right Side of Winch Cover

Seam Allowance Inside Winch Cover

Zigzag Stitching on Outside to Reinforce Seam

Fig 15

That's about all there is to it unless you want to add your boats name along the cover. The quickest way to do this is to cut the letters from insignia cloth. (Usually available from sailmakers in white, red or blue.) It is best to adjust the lettering and spacing between letters before you commit the self-adhesive insignia material to the cover.

Ensure the name will appear in a neat horizontal line. It is best to practise drawing the characters of the alphabet that you will need on paper before cutting the rather expensive sticky back material. If you do not have an artistic bent it is better to use capital letters only. If you are an artist you will not need me to tell you what imaginative and distinctive lettering and designs can be used. Figure 16 may be of some help.

SE A E ᴀGL E — How not to do it. The letter spacing is uneven and the characters have been cut to uneven sizes.

SEA EAGLE — Capital letters evenly spaced and level. Looks good.

FAST LADY — Italic capitals suggest speed and match the name.

CLOUD NINE — Capitals with serifs. More difficult to cut but they add a bit of class.

Shadowfax — The use of capitals and lower case letters.

Sweet Dream — Really fancy and quite difficult to cut and align - but elegant.

Fig 16

38

Most insignia material is better if it is ironed on (gentle heat) after its initial application. Do this as you would have done before the invention of the steam iron to press a pair of pants – i.e. lay a damp cloth over the cover and numbers before ironing.

You will now have a sail cover that you can be proud of because it looks good and because you made it yourself. It will be easy to put on and take off so it is worth using whenever the sail is lowered. The protection it affords should add years to the life of your mainsail. Try not to let sun or rain awnings rest on the sail-cover as they may chafe through where they touch it.

Photo 2. The final adjustment to a sail cover that will protect your sail for years.

Sail Bags

These should be large enough in width and depth, to hold a loosely packed sail.

If you leave a headsail hanked onto the forestay overnight or for any lengthy period, it should be bagged to protect it from UV and flying grit or dirt. With a suitable bag you can quickly stuff the clew in first (with sheets still attached and left protruding from the bag's mouth) followed by the bulk of the sail, pulling the bag up to the forestay where it can be secured and tied down by tightening the drawstring and making it off on the forestay with a quick-release knot. The carrying handle on the base of the bag can then be tied to the upper lifeline to hold the bag and sail clear of the deck. The halyard can be left attached and also secured by the drawstring.

This will mean that the headsail is ready for instant use in an emergency situation but looks neat and you have the confidence that you are protecting your sail.

Most sailbags that you buy or that come with the sail are made with a circle of cloth as a base sewn onto the body of the bag. The weight of the sail inside often causes that seam to split. For a stronger bag (and one that will fit more easily through a hatch) it is simpler to make it from one piece of cloth, with a square base.

If your hatch is not large enough to pass a sailbag through or if you do not stow the sails below, then it is better to have a shorter and wider bag that will make sail packing easier. Measurements will vary according to the size of the sail; however the finished size should be large enough for the sail to fit fairly loosely inside.

Photo 3. Here the sail is inside the bag, still hanked to the forestay and with sheets attached ready for an almost instant hoist.

Photo 4. Keeping the sail clear of the deck.

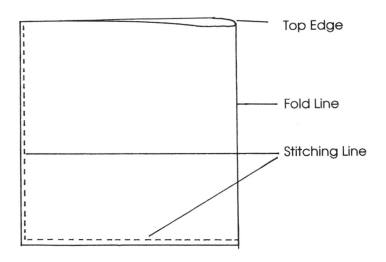

Fig 17

Take a length of cloth that measures the circumference of the finished bag and wide enough for one and a half times the required height. Fold it in half along the length and straight-stitch down the side and along the bottom. (See Figure 17)

For added strength press the seam allowances over and from the right side zigzag stitch along it a little to the side of the seam. Do not worry if you cannot sew right to the corner as this will not show.

Measure the bottom of the bag and divide by two. Crease the fold line or mark it with chalk. With the bag inside out, fold it across the corners, matching the bottom seam to the crease at one side and to the side seam at the other. Pin the seam lines and folds in place. (See Figure 18)

Take your halved measurement (for example we shall assume that it is 50cm) and, using a ruler or straight edge, measure 25cm each side of the centre seam to the fold. (See Figure 19)

Mark this line and stitch along it, tying off the ends.

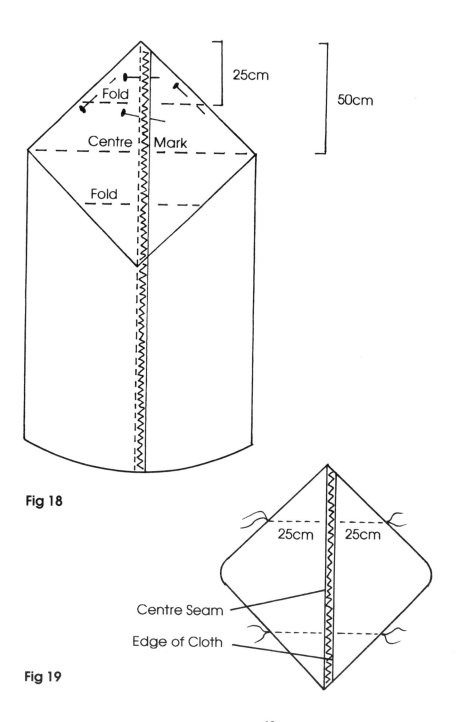

25cm

50cm

Fold

Centre | Mark

Fold

Fig 18

25cm | 25cm

Centre Seam

Edge of Cloth

Fig 19

Fig 20

Fold the corners to the middle, where they should
meet if the bag is to be a perfect square. Stitch
round them as in Figure 20.

For the drawstring at the top, mark a line round
the bag 1cm from the edge and another line 4cm
down from the first. Cut a patch 10cm by 4cm and
lay it on the inside of the bag with the long side
touching the second line and stitch round it. This
will reinforce the grommets through which the
drawstring emerges. Mark the position for the
grommets (No 1 size) 6cm apart and 1cm down
from the top of the patch and insert them. (See
Figure 21)

Crease along the first fold line round the bag,
then along the second one. Run the cord in through
one grommet, round the bag and out through the
other grommet and then knot the ends together.
Push the cord to the top of the hem so that it will
not catch in the machine and pin the hem down.
Stitch along the bottom of the hem. (See Figure 22)

44

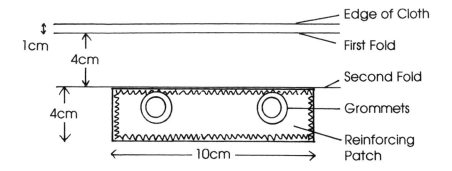

Edge of Cloth
First Fold
Second Fold
Grommets
Reinforcing Patch

1cm
4cm
4cm
10cm

Fig 21

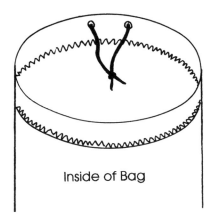

Inside of Bag

Fig 22

There are various ways of attaching a handle to the base of the bag.

1) The strongest handle is made by putting in a grommet at the centre of each triangle. Measure the distance between them and cut a strip of 2cm wide webbing to this length plus 15cm. Push the ends of the webbing through the grommets from the outside, taking care that it is not twisted, until you have 7cm emerging from each. Pin each end down away from the centre and stitch them in place. (See Figure 23)

Photo 5. A webbing handle emerging through grommets on the strong base of this sailbag.

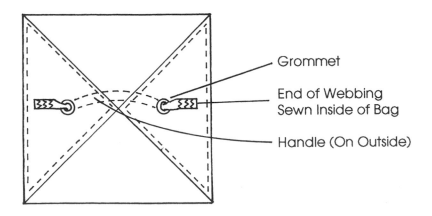

Grommet

End of Webbing
Sewn Inside of Bag

Handle (On Outside)

Fig 23

2) It is possible to use rope through the grommets, rather than webbing. Either tie the two ends together inside the bag or put a stopper knot at each end to stop them pulling through the grommets. This method does however, put a lot of strain on the grommets and they may pull out.

3) Webbing can simply be stitched to the base on the outside, but in this case you have no drain holes in the bottom of the bag in the event of having to stow a wet sail.

Any of the above methods can be used to make a side handle, but you will need to sew a reinforcing patch onto the inside of the bag first.

If you stow your sails below via a deck hatch, the bag can be made to fit by taking the measurement of the hatch opening and cutting the cloth to that length. In this case you will need to increase the height of the bag. Stitch as before, but for the corners use the measurements of two opposite sides. This way, if your hatch measures (for example) 55cm by 40cm you will end up with a rectangular base. Depending on which measurement you choose for the corners, they will either have a distance between them (Figure 24a) or overlap (Fig 24b).

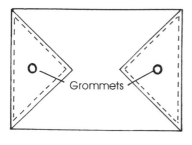

a

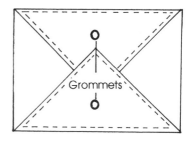

b

Fig 24a & b

To add that professional touch, you should consider marking the name of the sail that the bag will contain clearly on the outside. Using a waterproof marking pen and a stencil cut for fairly large letters, you can indicate if it contains for example 'NO 1 GENOA' or 'STORM JIB'. The practical aspect of this is self evident if you have guest or new crew aboard and adds to safety if you are unfortunate enough to be scrabbling about searching for the storm sails in rough conditions.

While on this topic another useful addition is the boat's name. It not only looks seamanlike, but may also prevent someone mistaking your sail for another if it happens to be in a sail loft or in storage somewhere.

Photo 6. The finished article

Sacrificial Strips – Roller-Furling Headsails

A roller furling headsail that is left hoisted (and furled) for most of the time, other than in use, requires some form of protection from UV degradation and airborne pollutants often found on the dockside and near ports. This protection can either be in the form of a 'sleeve' or 'sock' hoisted up over the sail, or more usually a 'sacrificial strip' stitched onto the sail and made from some form of UV resistant material.

In considering the fabric to use for the strip you should bear in mind the weight of the sailcloth from which your sail is made. (Either your sailmaker can tell you or you should know if you have made the sail.) Because the strip is attached to the leech of the sail, un-necessary weight is not desirable since in lighter airs it will tend to distort the aerodynamic shape of the sail. Therefore select a cloth weight that is below the weight of the sailcloth itself; the sacrificial strip bears no deliberate load and is there for protection only.

There are several sailcloth manufacturers who make UV retarding (Note not UV proof) sailcloth and also fabrics specially woven for other marine purposes where strong and prolonged exposure to UV can cause problems – Bimini Tops and awnings for example. It is best to seek advice on what is available, then you can also decide if you want your strip to be in colour, often dark blue (said to be less UV absorbent than other colours) but which you may consider does not enhance the appearance of the sail when set, or alternatively a fabric that matches as closely as possible the colour of your sail – often a creamy cotton colour.

It is easy enough to attach the strip yourself, though you may have to hand stitch through the head, clew and tack panels if you do not have access to a heavy duty sewing machine.

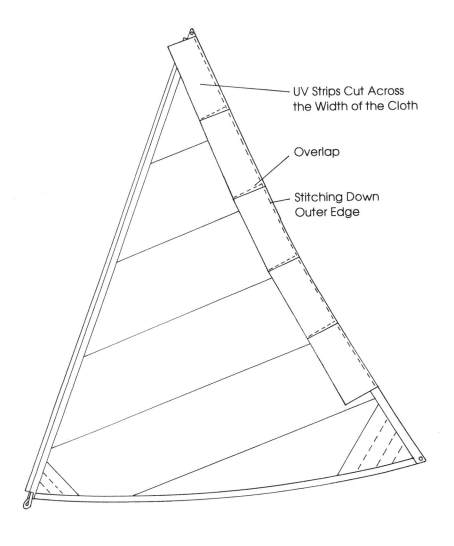

UV Strips Cut Across
the Width of the Cloth

Overlap

Stitching Down
Outer Edge

Fig 25

To work out how much material you will need, measure the length of the leech and divide this measurement by the width of the cloth. This will give you the number of strips to cut. For the width of the strips (from selvedge to selvedge) measure (at right angles to the leech) the exposed cloth when the sail is rolled and then add 10cm. Do the same for the foot of the sail, adding 5 – 8cm (depending on how tightly you furl it). Cut the strips across the width with a 'hot-knife' or flat bladed soldering iron to seal the edges, using a straight-edge rule or a metal strip to ensure an even cut.

When sewing the strip in place, make sure that you are applying it to the exposed side! The easiest way is to mark the clew when the sail is furled.

Starting at the head, lay the first strip down the leech, (if necessary pushing the leech-line to the centre of the tabling or hem) and stitch it as close to the edge as possible. Approximately 2cm before the selvedge, slide the next strip underneath and stitch over it; this will allow for the curve of the inverse roach and ensure that the inner edges of the strips will overlap. (See Figure 25)

Continue with each strip until you reach the clew. If your machine cannot handle the reinforced patches, these are not too difficult to do by hand. If the leech-line exits from a grommet and is made off to a cleat, trim the cloth so that it will lie neatly around these. (See Figure26)

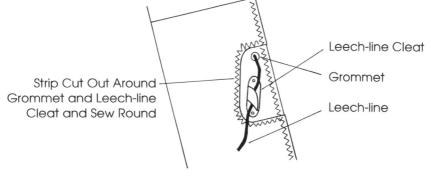

Strip Cut Out Around Grommet and Leech-line Cleat and Sew Round

Leech-line Cleat

Grommet

Leech-line

Fig 26

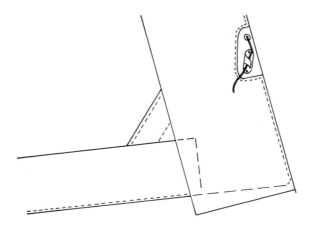

Fig 27

For the strip at the foot, slide the first panel just underneath the inner edge of the last leech panel, again aligning it with the edge. (See Figure 27)

Since the foot is likely to have an outward curve, the overlap at the edge need not be quite so much.

If you are not too sure of the shape of your sail, it may pay you to lay it out on a flat surface and place your strips onto it before you start sewing. In this case, you could stick them in place first to ensure that you get the correct tension.

Once you have stitched down the outer edge of the leech and the foot as far as you can by machine, it is advisable (both for extra strength and better shape) to over stitch the inner edge of the tabling. This will make the strip lie flatter and therefore easier to stitch down on the inner edge. If the leech strip is much wider than the 'arm' of your sewing machine, it is better to run a line of stitching down the centre of the strip before machining the inner edge. (See Figure 28)

Sew the inner edge in place, making sure that the tension of the strip matches that of the sail. Turn the sail round and stitch each join, being careful to leave enough space at the leech tabling for the leech-line to pass freely.

Photo 7. Genoa badly furled or strip too narrow.

At the head, clew and tack, trim of the excess material and either hand or machine stitch around the edges. If you have to hand stitch the outer edges of the strip through the reinforcement patches here, use a cross-stitch. (If necessary by punching holes first with a spike or nail.)
(See Figure 29)

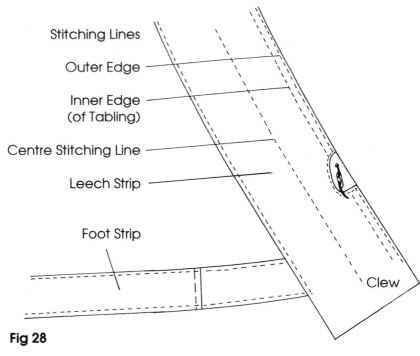

Stitching Lines

Outer Edge

Inner Edge
(of Tabling)

Centre Stitching Line

Leech Strip

Foot Strip

Clew

Fig 28

HEAD - Cut and stitch the strip to the edge
of the luff tape

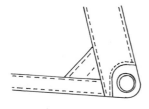

CLEW - Cut the cloth around the clew eye,
stitch around it, then trim the excess from
the foot and machine or hand-sew it to
the edge

TACK - Trim the material to
the edge of the luff tape
and machine along the
cut edge

Fig 29

Photo 8. Genoa correctly furled with an adequate width of sacrificial strip on the leech and foot.

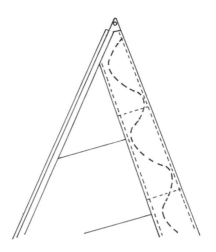

Fig 30

When the leech and foot strips are sewn in place, it is worth the extra time to reinforce them with a loosely curved line of stitching from edge to edge, head to clew and clew to tack. (See Figure 30)

If you are unlucky enough to damage the sacrificial strip, this stitching will prevent the wind from getting underneath and tearing the strip from the sail, which could cause further damage to both.

Chapter 2
Preventing Sail Damage

At some time when you are sitting comfortably in a harbour or marina, it is worth going over the sails, panel by panel and seam by seam, checking for holes, worn stitching, broken leech-lines and any evidence of chafe. If you find anything – ask yourself what caused it. In this way you may be able to save yourself work in the future. It's a might easier to repair a few broken stitches in harbour than to resew a whole seam at sea.

Mainsails and Mizzens

On a mainsail or mizzen, the first thing to check are the batten pockets. If they are worn at the ends, the batten may need new endcaps or rounding-off any sharp edges with a little sanding. Many sailmakers use elastic at the inner end of the pockets and if this has perished or slipped to one side, the batten could press against the end-stitching and weaken it.

For long distance blue-water cruising it is worthwhile considering a battenless mainsail, cut with a slightly inverse roach like a headsail. You will loose only a small amount of sail area, but I believe that this will be more than compensated for by the freedom from torn pockets and broken or lost battens. It also increases the ease of handling such a sail; it can be raised or lowered on any point of sailing, even if you are running downwind. Another advantage is that the leech is less likely to come into contact with the topping lift – another potential chafe area eliminated.

Some sailmakers are reluctant to build such a sail, but if you explain that you are cruising and not racing, you should be able to find one who will.

If you do not, as a matter of routine, cover a sail every time it is taken down, thread on the seams that are exposed to the sun will perish far faster than the sailcloth it is holding together. A quick check for weak stitching is to scratch the thread with a fingernail. If it starts to fray it is suspect. Watch particularly for where the sail chafes on the shrouds when running. You can usually see where this occurs by a dirty line down the sail (or two or three, depending on how many reefs you have and how often you use them). If the sail is fairly new and clean, it is possible to prevent the thread wearing out by sticking a patch over the seam on each side and then replacing it periodically.

Seams and Leech

The seams are particularly vulnerable from the leech to about 30cm into the body of the sail. Even if there is no apparent sign of wear it is worth running a line of stitching down the centre of the seam at this point (taking care not to sew through the leech-line). If the sail has only two rows of stitching, it is worth having a third line put down the centre of every seam along the entire length.

If the leech is turned over and only stitched on the inside of the tabling, the leech-line will chafe the stitching on the inside of the seams, creating a weak point at which the seam could start to open. This can be prevented by running another line of stitching down the outside edge to reinforce the leech, especially at the seams. (See Figure 31)

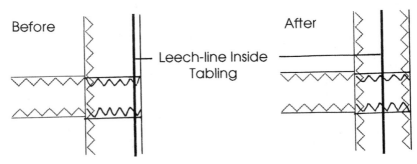

Before ┤ After ┤

Leech-line Inside Tabling ┤

Fig 31

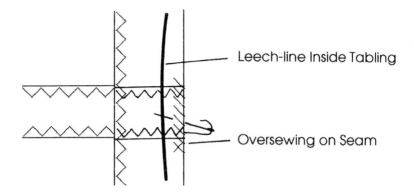

Leech-line Inside Tabling

Oversewing on Seam

Fig 32

If the leech is not wide enough to let you do this by machine, it is worth making the effort to oversew the seam join together with a crisscross stitch – this will strengthen the critical points.
(See Figure 32)

A frequent cause of broken leech-lines is the metal grommet through which they emerge. I find it better to remove the grommet with a pair of pliers or snips (making sure that the backing washer is extracted as well) and to sew a piece of webbing or doubled sail tape over the leech tabling to protect the hole. (See Figure 33)

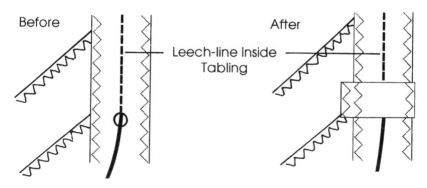

Before

After

Leech-line Inside Tabling

Fig 33

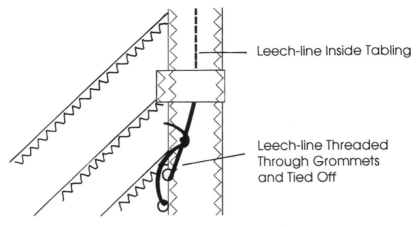

Leech-line Inside Tabling

Leech-line Threaded
Through Grommets
and Tied Off

Fig 34

Leech-line cleats are effective if they are the
jamming kind that are set into the sail a little way,
but if they are the kind that slot over the edge of
the leech, they often crack along the spine and are
then unusable. In this case it is better to remove
them, reinforce the hole with webbing as in Figure
33, and put two grommets (10cm apart and 2.5cm
from the edge of the sail) just below the webbing to
thread the line through. (See Figure 34)

Mast Slides

Shackled-on slides are another frequent problem.
The shackle is constantly working back and forth,
so it can chew a hole in the luff rope in a
surprisingly short time, particularly if a metal
shackle is used. The plastic shackles that many
sailmakers use have a limited life due to wear and
UV exposure.

A far better method is to attach the slides with
two or three turns of 15cm webbing, stitched
through itself and through the luff rope. (Figure 35)
The advantage is that when it wears through it is
easy to replace without removing the sail from the
mast or boom.

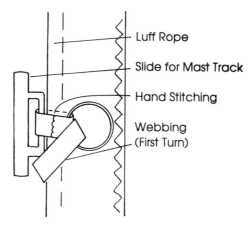

Luff Rope

Slide for Mast Track

Hand Stitching

Webbing
(First Turn)

Fig 35

Eyes and Cringles

Tack, clew and head eyes, together with reef cringles can present a problem, especially if they are pressed in with aluminium rings. Aluminium will eventually corrode in salt water or a salt air environment and the cloth underneath will be eaten away. These aluminium rings should be replaced before you leave port because when the cloth has been attacked, then the eye will have to be replaced by a much larger one to fit the bigger hole – or even worse, the entire patch will have to be replaced if the hole has spread too close to the corner of the sail.

If these eyes are the sewn-in type, with brass rings and liners, excessive strain can distort them and occasionally break the ring. If the eye is not completely circular it is an indication that it is reaching breaking point and a remedy is needed. Even if it appears normal, a good precaution is to add support by running a length of 25cm webbing through the eye and then stitching it back-to-back through the patch. You may well have to do this by hand if your sewing machine is not up to sewing through reinforcement patches. The webbing can be glued in place with a few spots of clear contact

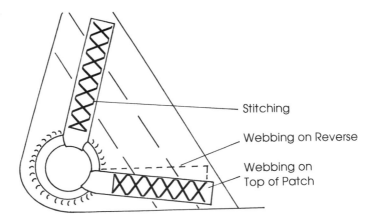

Stitching

Webbing on Reverse

Webbing on
Top of Patch

Fig 36

cement first to achieve the correct tension (the
webbing should pull hard against the ring) and to
keep it in position for stitching. (See Figure 36)

If the reef patches on the leech are staggered on
the long edge but are several layers thick on the
short edge, then you have a potential danger spot
because three or more layers of cloth present a
single edge to the main sailcloth of the sail can
present a cutting edge. This situation can be
rectified by unpicking the threads on the short side
and trimming off the layers of cloth under the cover
patch, retstitching each layer as you go. (See Figure
37) If necessary reinforce the outer layer with a
strip of sail tape over the edge and into the sail. The
luff reef patches are not so critical as they have the
support of the luff rope and are not subjected to the
flogging that the leech often gets.

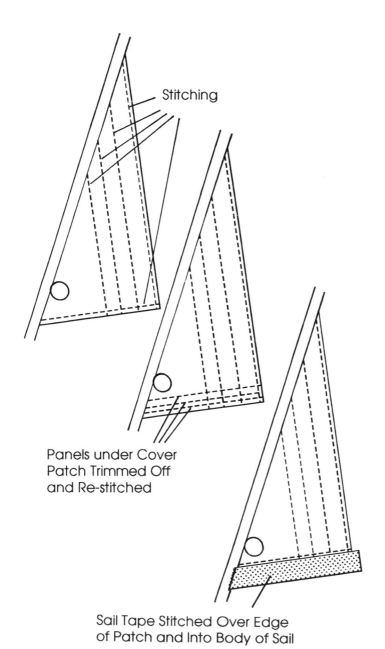

Stitching

Panels under Cover
Patch Trimmed Off
and Re-stitched

Sail Tape Stitched Over Edge
of Patch and Into Body of Sail

Fig 37

Headboard

Headboards should be examined carefully. If they are riveted, check that the rivets are still sound and that they pass through the board each side and through the head patch. A rivet can often look solid on one side but may be disintegrating on the other, or even be broken where it passes through the sail.

If you find one or two like this, it is a fair bet that the rest are also likely to fail. In this event, drill all the rivets out and either replace them (if the holes are not too large) with a pop-rivet or rivet gun. Alternatively stitch them together, following the same holes with doubled heavy waxed thread and a sailmaker's needle. (See Figure 38)

Check that the eye in the headboard has not been worn by the shackle on the mainsail halyard. If it has started to wear or distort you may have to replace the entire headboard because once it has torn out, taking the cloth with it, you will have no method of hoisting the mainsail. (It is worth carrying a couple of spare headboards of the same size – just in case.)

Remember that metal on metal will wear. Spare headboards, if not available locally, can be made from 3-4mm aluminium sheet or 2-3mm stainless steel sheet depending on the weight of the sail. Do not forget that you need a plate for each side of the sail. Tufnol, if you can still find it, is good and in an emergency you can even resort to fibre-glassed plywood although it will need to be considerably thicker and will not last too long.

Check to see that the headboard slides are securely fastened. There should be two – one immediately below the halyard eye and a second near the lower corner to prevent the headboard twisting and possibly jamming when the sail is hoisted.

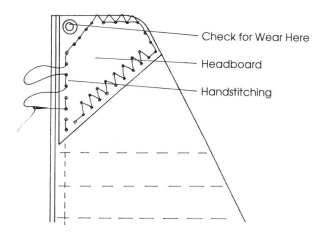

Check for Wear Here

Headboard

Handstitching

Fig 38

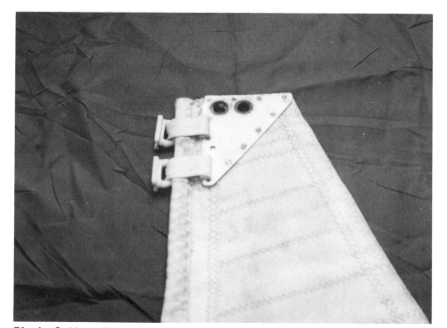

Photo 9. Here the two headboard slides are attached by webbing. A good alternative to shackels since the wear is less than metal to metal.

Headsails

Head and Tack Eyes

The first thing to check on a hanked headsail is the luff wire. If it is galvanised, bend the eye at the head and tack back and forth to make sure it is not broken. The most likely place for failure is either just below or above the swage. If it feels sound, you could leave it. If not, replace it with stainless wire.

If the sail is in good condition, I would replace a galvanised luff wire with stainless anyway, since this is a job that is more easily done in a sail loft or in harbour than at sea.

The eye at the head of the sail will almost certainly be lashed to a grommet in the patching, but often the eye in the tack is simply stitched to the sail and could easily pull out under stress. If this is the case, I would advise you to put in a grommet about 50cm above the eye and lash it securely . (See Figure 39) Additional strength can be gained by running a strip of webbing along the foot, through the eye and back along the other side of the sail, hand stitching it in place as shown in Figure 36.

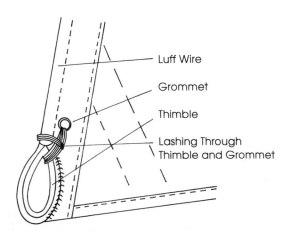

Fig 39

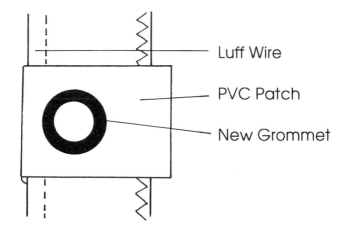

Luff Wire

PVC Patch

New Grommet

Fig 40

Hanks

These are the next areas to examine. If there are no protective patches under the hanks, the cloth over the luff wire will quickly wear through, especially with the knock-on hanks that most sailmakers currently favour.

You can cut out a thin strip of PVC or thin leather, slide it under the hank and seize the ends round the luff wire. However, it is better to remove the hank, take out the grommet and put in a new one through a PVC patch round the luff.

(See Figure 40)

Knock-on hanks can be re-used a couple of times provided that they are removed carefully. This is possible by the use of a cold chisel and a mallet over a block of wood with a hole in the centre. Position the chisel over the opening and tap gently until the opening is wide enough to slip the hank off the luff wire.

Sew-on hanks take more time to put on but are obviously re-usable as often as you like and are occasionally found second-hand in sail lofts if new ones are not available. If they are worn where they rub on the forestay, which generally happens towards the head of the sail, the most likely reason is that the luff is not tensioned correctly. It is the luff wire that should take the main tension and the hanks should be treated as attachments rather than supports.

If you find yourself far from the nearest stockist it is worth swapping the worst worn from the head of the sail with the more solid ones nearer the tack. Like spare battens, a supply of spare hanks is well worth carrying aboard.

Chafe Patches

You will probably find a dirty mark on the foot of low cut headsails such as the genoa, near the tack where the sail passes over the pulpit or lifeline when sailing off the wind. This can be remedied, if the sail is not cut to full forestay length, by hoisting the sail with a wire pendant between tack and deck tack-point, sufficiently long to keep the foot above the cause of the problem. You will not lose sail area by this addition but will be flying the sail a little higher, which is usually desirable when reaching or running – the points of sailing when the chafe occurs.

Most genoas are cut to full forestay length and in this case your only alternative is to apply chafe patches on either side of the sail to protect it. The simplest method is to use white iron-on insignia cloth with a single line of stitching round the edge. (See Figure 41)

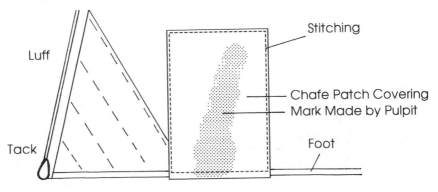

Fig 41

Photo 10. A low-cut headsail needs protection in the form of a chafe patch where it rubs over the life-lines or pulpit.

Photo 11. Flown on a tack pendant, it clears the hazard.

You can use the same cure where a headsail rubs against the spreaders and shrouds. The addition of spreader-boots or taped sponge around the spreader tips is also a useful prevention above; and lower down, a split length of nylon tube forced over the shrouds will prevent chafe when beating and tacking into wind. Unless you have a classic boat and are searching for an aesthetic look, baggywrinkle is time consuming to apply and adds considerable windage where you need it least.

Leech Seam Ends

If the sail has a tabling which has been cut off the sail, creased to form a hem and then stitched back on, check that the leech-line has not worn through the stitching inside. Once the leech starts to go, it is amazing in just how short a time it may take for the sail to tear right across – and how much harder to repair it! Take the time to sew a small reinforcing patch over the end of each seam. (See Figure 42)

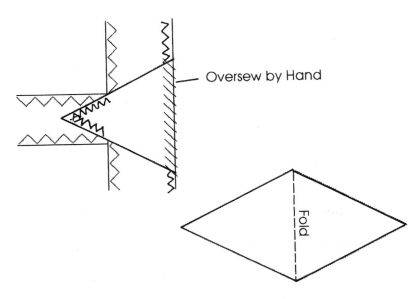

Oversew by Hand

Fold

Fig 42

Clew

The clew eye takes a great deal of strain, so examine it to see that the stitching on the panels is sound. Shackles used to attach the headsail sheets to the sail can cause considerable wear to the liner of the eye. They are best avoided and a bowline is entirely preferable – especially since a clout round the ear from a bowline is less painful than a flying lump of metal.

If the clew eye or ring is showing signs of distortion, it can be strengthened by running strips of webbing through it and hand stitching them back to back (See Fig 36) with the addition of an extra strip in the middle. (Along the mitre if that is the cut of the sail.)

Roller Furling Headsails

Check the luff tape along its entire length. Look especially closely at the head and tack. If it is worn through in one or more spots, mark the positions with masking tape or similar and hoist the sail. Now for a trip aloft to see what is causing the damage. A frequent problem area is where the sections of track fit together – check for perfect alignment. The top and bottom of the luff tape will wear through if the edges of the track are not completely smooth and rounded off – easy to remedy with a fine file.

The sacrificial strip, which is a *must* on a roller furling headsail, should be checked at least once a year, especially if the leech edge does not go over the tabling and attach to the reverse side of the sail. Ideally, this strip should attach to the inner edge of the tabling on the reverse side first, then be folded over the leech to the right side, stitched down the outer edge of the leech, and then sewn to the sail along the inner edge of the strip. If this method is used, when exposed thread perishes, there will still be a line of sound stitching underneath.

UV resistant material, such as acrylic should be used. See page 28 for more information.

Spinnakers and Cruising Chutes.

Check along every seam for pulled stitching. Often, if the thread has caught on something it will pull out in a loop without breaking (since the material is soft), causing the sail to pucker. It is possible, using a heavy needle or even a toothpick, to ease the thread back into place, getting rid of the loop and retensioning the stitching.

Look for small tears in the nylon. Most of these can be treated with self adhesive spinnaker repair material which is very easy to apply.

Photo 12. The basics of a pretty comprehensive sail repair kit.

Chapter 3
The Basic Sail Repair Kit

Buying a ready made sail repair kit from a chandler or by mail-order is easy, especially since they come in a variety of handy Ditty Bags – but if you were to forget the 'packaging' and price out the individual items, you are likely to find that you could do better buying each item separately. By studying your sails and your boat, you will learn what to carry with you and what is of most use to you, rather than buying a fancy pack that is likely to include a lot of items you will never use. If you are lucky enough to live near a second-hand boat store or go to 'boat jumbles', or have a friendly sailmaker and keep your eyes open for useful items, you will soon put a kit together. The Ditty Bag you can make yourself!

Obviously, if you have the money to spare, a sewing machine is first on the list. This does not necessarily have to be a purpose designed sail makers machine, although a model such as the 'Reed's Sailmaker' is a worthwhile investment. (Do buy from a reputable source, since I have experienced purchasing a machine with a false label which proved totally inferior to the genuine model it purported to be.) The older 'Singer' machines can be found in second-hand shops and are entirely suitable. If you are shopping for a machine, carry a sample of the sailcloth that you will be working on and insist on a demonstration to ensure that it is up to the job. To sew sails, you will need to be able to use a No14 or 16 needle and increase the foot pressure to the maximum weight.

Provision for a hand-crank is a must, but if you have a generator on board, (240V or 110V) it is worth getting the equivalent motor. Finding a 12V motor can be difficult but the 'Jabsco Water Puppy' water pump motor will fit most, if not all, domestic machines. Carry spare belts, spare needles and spare bobbins with you. In the case of the last two, they should be kept in an airtight container with a drop of machine oil to prevent rust.

Having a sewing machine on board and knowing how to use it, is a way of earning money while you are cruising; practise on your own sails first though! There are many yachts that do not have the space for a sewing machine and whose owners are only too happy to find someone to fix their sails.

Other items

Two big spools of *machine thread*, polyester such as Dacron; V69 is an average weight that will run through a domestic machine easily with a No 14 or 16 needle.

A *sailmaker's palm* is a necessity. These can be bought for either right or left hands.

A selection of mixed *sail needles*, which must be kept in an airtight container with a little oil to prevent rust.

A large spool of *waxed hand-sewing thread* which will also replace all those little reels of whipping twine; the wax will make it stick to whatever you are trying to whip when you pull it tight, unlike other twine which has a tendency to spring free unless you keep the pressure on.

A good sharp pair of *scissors* (kept hidden so that they cannot be blunted by cutting rope, wire, patches for the inflatable or the occasional haircut).

Webbing. At least 20m of 1.5cm(half inch) webbing for sewing on slides.

10m of 2.5cm(1 inch) webbing for reinforcing tack, clew and reef eyes.

Sail Tape. Sailmaking suppliers call this 'split sailcloth' and it can be bought in a variety of weights and widths.

20m of the widest you can find. (Possibly 15cm)

20m of lighter thinner tape. (About 8cm)

5 rolls of *wide masking tape* – invaluable for holding a sail together and getting it into shape

before you repair it. Also for holding a patch onto the sail – peel it off as you sew.

A *hot-knife* or *soldering iron* to cut sailcloth patches and seal the edges of torn cloth; also good for sealing rope ends.

6 *stainless steel D-ring*s – the easiest way to replace a torn-out eye at the clew, head or tack of a sail. Also useful for emergency repairs to reef cringles.

A box of *No 2 brass grommets and washers* and the tools to insert them; for slides, hanks and reef points. Most sailmakers use No1 grommets, so if one of these has pulled out, tearing the hole slightly, the larger size will generally hold secure without the necessity for a patch underneath.

Spare *sew-on hanks* – many sailmakers have old ones from sails that have been converted for roller furling and will sell them at a reasonable price.

Spare *battens* – buy a length of batten material and cut it to size as necessary. If you do not have the space to carry a full length (about 3m), cut it into strips the size of the longest batten, you can then cut them further as the need arises.

Spare *headboards* – and rivets to install them (also a *pop-rivet gun*) are worth carrying. (The rivet gun, with an assortment of extra rivets will prove its worth in many ways other than sailmaking. It can be used to apply mast and boom fittings for example.)

Spare *sailcloth* – any scraps you can beg or buy that are roughly the same weight as your sails will be handy.

Spinnaker repair tape – one reel of each colour that is in your spinnaker or chute.

Now for some not-so-obvious things that will not be found in the average commercial sail repair kit.

2m of white *insignia cloth* (or the nearest colour to match your sails). Most sailmakers carry stock.

A *travel iron* – or an old *flat iron* that can be heated on a stove.

3 large *seam rippers* (unpickers) – the small domestic ones are not strong enough for sails. Available from 'Singer' shops or sailmaker's suppliers.

A heavy *rawhide mallet* – from sailmaker's suppliers.

A large office-type *stapler* and spare *staples*.

5 rolls of *double-sided* adhesive tape.

2 reels of *silver duct tape* or *adhesive carpet tape*.

Clear *contact adhesive*.

Spool of 3mm *braided leech-line* or soft cord.

Scraps of *leather* or *PVC*.

Assortment of household darning needles – the shorter the better.

Several packets of *waxed dental floss*.

Sewing machine oil or silicone spray.

Soft plastic or wooden *cutting board*.

Packet of *pushpins* or *drawing pins*.

This might seem like a lot of extra weight to carry on a small yacht, but packed carefully these items will not take up much space, except for the sewing machine – but without that, you will need infinite patience!

Chapter 4
Sail Repairs at Sea

Repairing sails at sea is not an easy job and is generally done under the worst possible conditions. In a Force Eight gale (or worse) most of your attention is concentrated on hanging on, staying upright and hopefully getting somewhere. The fact that a few stitches in the leech of your jib have broken may well pass un-noticed. Under these conditions the problem may only come to light when the sail tears right across and starts to flog itself to shreds.

With the growing popularity of roller-furling, many yachts carry perhaps only one other headsail, probably a storm jib and if that too becomes damaged it leaves the yacht semi- immobilized apart from recourse to the engine. Sods Law will of course rule and it is highly likely that the 'iron topsail' will decide to go on strike.

So here are some ideas on how to do basic 'get yourself out of trouble' repairs at sea. Later, we shall go into ways of turning your instant repair into a more professional job once you have reached the safety and calm of a harbour – but for now, let's concentrate on getting you there.

For stitching repairs I use a darning needle (the smaller the better) and dental floss, (rather than waxed thread, which requires a three-sided sailmaker's needle). The darning needle will pass more easily through the original stitching holes without tearing a larger hole in the cloth and dental floss is much stronger than the original machine thread, although almost as fine.

Leech Repairs

1) If you are lucky enough to catch the jib with part of the leech stitching gone, before the damage has spread into the body of the sail, it is a simple enough job to oversew the tabling back on the outer edge and tack it down on the inner edge, following the original stitching holes but using only about every third one.

2) If the leech-line has broken it should be repaired, however roughly, as this can help to hold the sail together. Feel with your finger where the ends are and unpick just enough of the stitching to enable you to hook out each end. If there is not enough slack at the clew for the two ends to join, a length of 3mm cord can be threaded through with a straightened out coat-hanger (using pliers, turn the end over to form a narrow eye). Tie the ends of the cord together with a flat enough knot to enable the line to move freely in the tabling (or, if the turn-over is very narrow, you may have to sew the ends together – see Fig 43), and then restitch the part you unpicked.

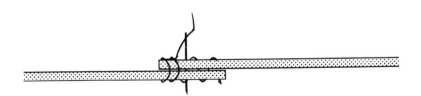

Stitch through the cord then round
teach side and back through the centre.

Fig 43

3) If the sail has started to tear along a seam, due to the thread wearing out, for a quick repair tack through the inner line of stitching holes on each side of the seam, making sure that you do not catch the leech-line with the thread (see Figure 44).

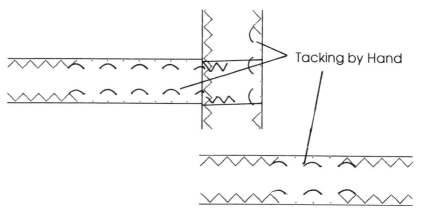

Tacking by Hand

Fig 44

Torn Sailcloth

4) If the sailcloth itself is torn, but only a short tear in the body of the sail, the edges can be brought together with a herringbone stitch. (See Figure 45)

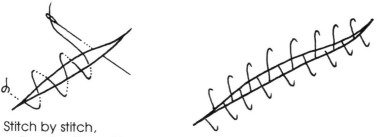

Stitch by stitch,
pull on the thread to bring the edges of the tear together.

Fig 45

For a longer or L-shaped tear, provided the cloth is still sound, the same method can be used but should be reinforced with an iron on patch of insignia cloth over one side.

5) If the tear extends from the edge to some distance into the body of the sail, the quickest instant repair is to herringbone it roughly to keep the shape, then onto a dry sail stick a length of duct tape or carpet tape along the tear on both sides of the sail. If time permits, tack along the edge around the tape. Otherwise with the staple gun opened and a so ft board underneath, staple the duct tape to the sail at 8cm intervals. Turn the sail over and bend the staples down; repeat the process on this side between the original staples so that they are alternately facing and reversed. To reinforce the edge, cut a strip of 1.5 cm (half inch) webbing to extend 20cm either side of the tear, sealing the ends with a match or lighter, fold it in half and oversew it to the outer edge of the sail. (See Figure 46)

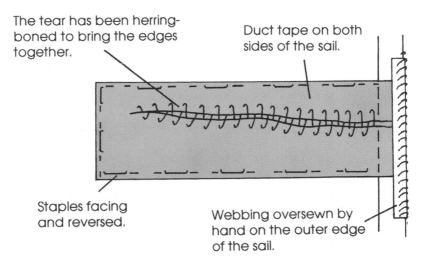

The tear has been herring-boned to bring the edges together.

Duct tape on both sides of the sail.

Staples facing and reversed.

Webbing oversewn by hand on the outer edge of the sail.

Fig 46

Frayed Leech

6) If the greater part of the leech is frayed due to flogging, try an 'instant recut'. Trim the frayed edge off and fold it over, then staple a length of folded sail tape down it, tack along the inner edge and oversew the outer edge. This will not improve the shape of the sail but will help hold it together until you can do a proper repair.

Clew and Tack Repairs

7) If the eye at the clew or tack corrodes or tears out, rather than replacing it (into already weakened cloth) it will be far stronger and more effective to repair it with a stainless steel D-ring or round ring.

If you are using a D-ring (Figure 47), lay the ring onto the cloth so that the outer edge of the straight side is touching the innermost part of the damaged cloth. Draw a pencil line along the outer edge of the ring, and cut along this line with a sharp knife. If possible, heat seal the edge with a soldering iron or sharp knife to prevent fraying. Mark a stitching line in 5mm from the cutting line and oversew the ring to the sail, using a heavy sailmaker's needle and doubled waxed thread. If the patch is very thick, it is easier to punch holes for the needle first, using a mallet and awl – or a long nail – over a soft board.

Then cut three strips of 2.5cm (1 inch) webbing, long enough to lie back to back through the ring and extend at least 15cm into the sail. Stick these down with a little clear contact glue to ensure the correct tension (the straps should pull the ring tight into the sail so that there is no strain on the hand stitching) and then sew by hand each strap through the sail to its other half on the reverse side.

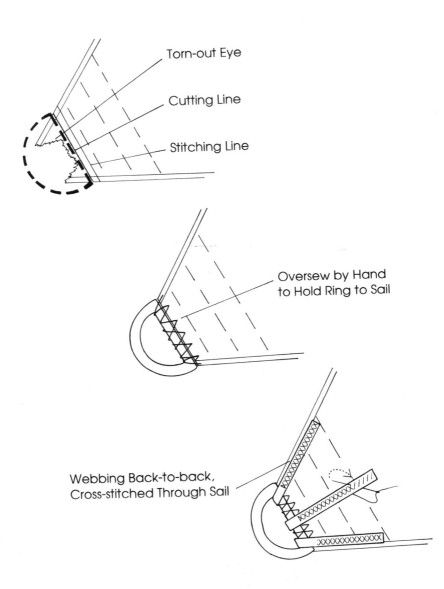

Fig 47

If you do not have a D-ring large enough to fit across the corner, a round ring can be used (See Figure 48) provided that it will fit into the place left by the old one. The same method of attachment should be used.

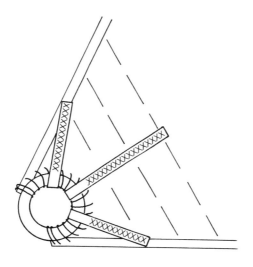

Fig 48

If the head eye has torn out it can be repaired in the same way but only two strips of webbing will be necessary, one down the luff and one down the leech.

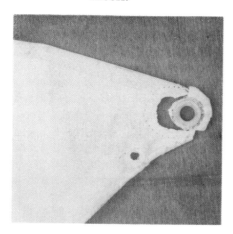

Photo 13.
In a case like this, it is often better to start anew with a D-ring.

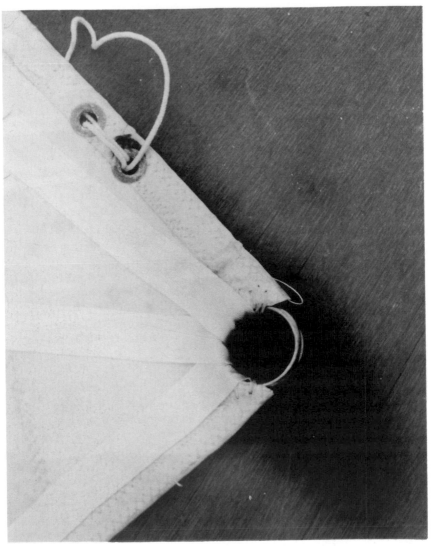

Photo 14. A round ring used as an emergency repair to the clew of this sail

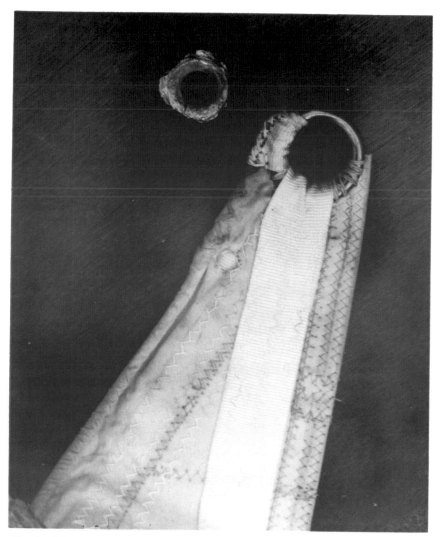

Photo 15. A replacement round ring sewn into the head of this sail. Note the eye it replaces.

Damaged Reef Points

8) On a mainsail or mizzen that has slab or jiffy reefing, keep an eye on the reef points. If one should tear, the sail is still usable provided that the grommet is removed and the tear patched (however roughly) to stop it spreading. Use iron-on insignia cloth, duct tape or spinnaker repair tape (both the latter will have to be tacked into place round the edge). One less tie will make no difference and more damage will be caused by using a tie through a torn out grommet.

Torn out reef points are most often caused by fastening the reef ties too tightly. They are designed only to hold the redundant body of the sail in place and should be tied as loosely as possible. The strain on the sail is taken from the reef tack and clew.

If the tear on a reef point is too extensive, it is better to shorten sail to the next reef (if you have one!) until conditions permit a proper repair to be effected.

Broken Battens

9) If a batten breaks and you have no replacement, remove it as quickly as possible. The broken ends, if left in the pocket, will do far more damage to the sail than the flapping leech will sustain. (Tighten up the leech-line to prevent the leech flogging too much.)

If a batten starts to wear through its pocket, a strip of duct tape stuck over the worn spot and tacked or stapled through the stitching will hold it in place.

Broken Slides

10) If a slide breaks on the luff it is no great problem. One or two missing, so long as they are not consecutive, will not matter. However, if they are towards the head of the sail, it is worthwhile when conditions permit, to drop the sail and move one or two from the lower part of the luff to replace them. The empty grommets can then, if necessary, be used to hold a lashing around the mast at a point that is easy to reach. (See Figure 49)

Mainsail Foot Repair

11) If the foot of the sail is attached to the boom by means of round plastic slugs (or slides, depending on the type of track in your boom) these can also break, depending on how much wear and exposure to the sun they have had. Rather than leave the foot of the sail unattached, it is possible to lash it through the grommets and round the boom with a light line (3mm leech-line is ideal), thus taking some of the strain off the remaining slugs. (See Figure 49)

12) If the foot of the sail has a bolt rope that runs through a groove in the boom, the stitching at the edge of the tabling or tape round the rope can be a weak spot when the sail flogs. If it tears along the foot, there is very little that can be done about it at sea in bad weather except to reef the sail before the damage spreads. If the sail is roller-reefed round the boom, at least two turns should be taken to ensure it doesn't tear any further.

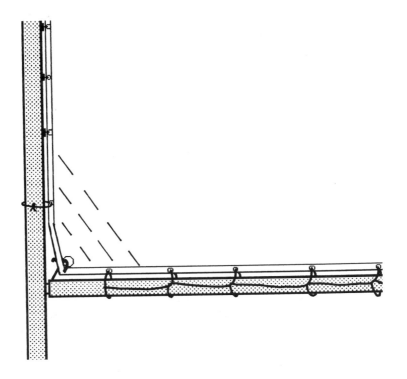

Fig 49

I *must* emphasize that most of these repairs are
strictly temporary measures, which with luck, will
get you out of trouble. As soon as you reach port
they should be repaired properly. If you are
fortunate you may find a sailmaker who can be
relied on but in many remote places the 'sailmaker'
is the local shoe maker or an unqualified amateur.
Check samples of his work and enquire about his
prices before you entrust your sail to him. Often
you will find that you can do the job better and
more cheaply yourself.

The next chapter will give you some ideas on how
to turn your temporary repairs into permanent
ones.

Chapter 5
Repair Your Own Sails

Let us assume that you have experienced some bad weather and have been forced into making emergency repairs as described in the previous chapter or that you have observed a major problem on a sail that demands a permanent solution. You have arrived at your destination and wish to carry out the sail repairs properly and be ready for sea in a short period.

The first task is to clean and dry the sail to be repaired. If it is not possible to wash the entire sail, then you must at least wash those areas of the sail to be attended. Sail tape, insignia cloth and double-sided tape will all adhere far better to a dry, clean and salt-free sailcloth – besides which the sail is far more pleasant to work on and the salt will not penetrate the sewing machine.

I shall run through the same list of instant repairs as numbered in the previous chapter and assume that you do not have the use of a zigzag sewing machine.

If you do have a zigzag machine, most of these repairs will take considerably less time. It may be worthwhile to find such a machine that you could borrow or to take the sail, tacked into shape, to someone ashore who would be prepared to sew it on a machine for you. In the latter case, pack the sail into a bag with the parts to be stitched on top. This will mean that you do not have to spread the entire sail in a possibly limited space.

Leech Repairs

1) Torn Leech. This is a simple matter of running two lines of stitching down the leech tabling. Leave your emergency stitching in place and sew over it. This will prevent the tabling from slipping.

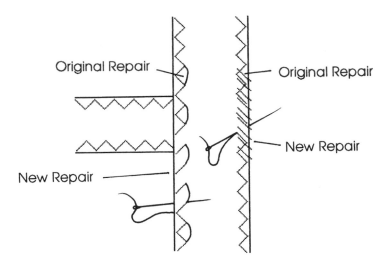

Original Repair

Original Repair

New Repair

New Repair

Fig 50

To repair broken stitching by hand (See Figure 50), use a darning needle and dental floss, following the original stitching holes. This can be turned into a professional looking job by going back under the first line of stitching to produce the zigzag look. Be sure to take the repair stitching a little way into the sound thread on each side.

2) Broken Leech-line.
If you were forced to tie the ends of the leech-line together for a quick repair, it should be untied and stitched (See Fig 43) and the tabling restitched as in Figure 50.

3) Torn Seam
Restitch the seam, leaving your original repair in place to make sure that the tension stays equal on both layers of cloth. Use the same method as in Figure 50, matching the stitching holes to ensure the sail keeps its original shape. If you take it to be sewn on a machine, trim off any knots in your hand sewing as they could cause a machine to jam.

If the selvedge of the sailcloth has started to fray, it should be reinforced before the seam is repaired. Should it only be one or two threads along the edge that have to come out, it will be sufficient to heat seal the edge before restitching, but if the frayed edge extends further into the seam than this, a reinforcing patch will have to be applied.

There are two ways of doing this. The easiest method, (especially without a sewing machine) is to leave your tacking down the inner line of stitching, trim off any knots and then to put a patch of iron-on cloth or sail tape on each side of the sail, overlapping the frayed part of the seam by 3cm, matching both sides. If using sail tape, this can be stapled or stuck (preferably with double-sided tape) in place to make it easier to stitch. To obtain the zigzag effect, mark a light pencil line just inside the edge of the patch and another one 5mm inside this as a sewing guide line. (See Figure 51)

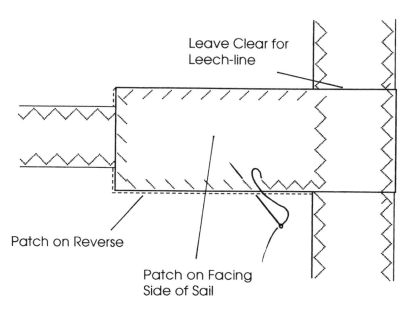

Leave Clear for
Leech-line

Patch on Reverse

Patch on Facing
Side of Sail

Fig 51

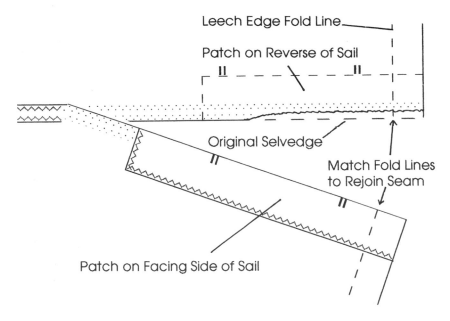

Leech Edge Fold Line

Patch on Reverse of Sail

Original Selvedge

Match Fold Lines
to Rejoin Seam

Patch on Facing Side of Sail

Fig 52

The alternative method is to reinforce both layers
of cloth. To do this you must undo your original
repair and strengthen them both with a strip of sail
tape, the edge of which should lie level with the
original selvedge and extend a little way into the
panel. You can then resew the seam as it was
before, making sure that the tension is equal. The
easiest way to do this is to pin the cloth to a
wooden board (or to the jetty) with push pins and
either sticking it together or by making pencil tack
marks across the two layers of cloth. (See Figure
52)

Match up the leech ends of the two panels and
pin them together at the fold line of the tabling.
Stretch the sail gently towards the luff and when
the two panels seem evenly tensioned, either pin or
stick them together (using double-sided tape), and
sew along each 'selvedge' with a zigzag stitch.

Restitch the leech as in No1 (Torn Leech) and
reinforce as shown in Figure 42.

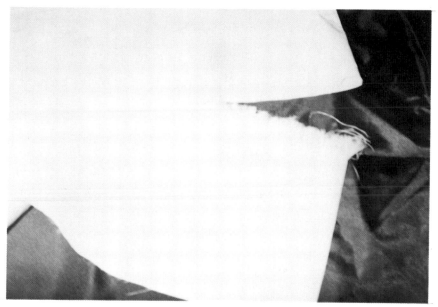

Photo 16. The badly frayed selvedge in this torn seam means reinforcing as shown in Fig 52.

Photo 17. The strip of sail tape. Its edge is level with the original selvedge.

Photo 18. The finished repair. (Coloured sail tape is only for clarification.)

Torn Sailcloth

4) The best method of turning this into a professional looking job is to remove the herringbone stitching (and if used, the iron-on patch) and press the sail with a warm iron so that it lies flat. To keep the edges of the long tear together, stick a wide piece of masking tape to the reverse side. Then cut a thin strip of iron-on insignia cloth the length of the tear, peel off the paper backing and stick it onto the side facing you. Press it on with a warm iron over a thin cloth. Cut two larger pieces of the same material back to back, of a size to extend 5cm above, below and each end of the tear. Mark a rough guideline in pencil on the sail 5cm above and from one end of the tear and stick one patch to this line. Turn the sail over, remove the masking tape and hold the sail to the light so that the outline of the large patch is visible.

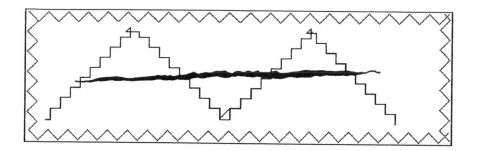

Fig 53

Trace around this in light pencil to give the
position for the second patch. Press this into place
and iron both sides. (If you iron over a cloth, the
glue on the insignia cloth will not stick to the iron.)
Stitch round the patch using the zigzag look alike
stitch as before. If the sail is very heavy, it may be
necessary to double the patches on both sides and
to stitch back and forth across it. (See Figure 53)

5) Tear From The Leech Into The Body Of The Sail
Remove all your emergency repair including the
webbing. Unpick the leech back to 25cm each side
of the tear and press the sail flat. (Also the tabling if
it is a fold-over hem.) On a wooden board (or jetty)
pin out the sail, lining up the tabling fold lines, with
the edges of the tear together. Position the pins as
close to the edge of the sail as possible. Now gently
stretch the sail along the tear until it lies flat and
the tension is equal on both sides; pin the sail
down either side of the inner edge of the tear. (See
Figure 54)
Cut a thin strip of insignia cloth to run the length
of the tear up to the edge of the sail and press this
in place to hold the tear together. Cut two back to
back patches to extend 5cm around and beyond the
tear. Before sticking the facing one, lay it on the

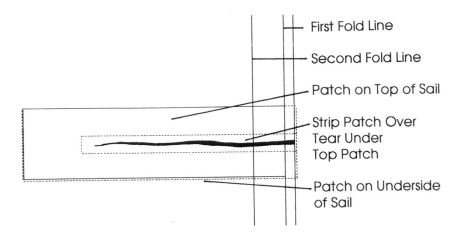

First Fold Line

Second Fold Line

Patch on Top of Sail

Strip Patch Over
Tear Under
Top Patch

Patch on Underside
of Sail

Fig 54

cloth and trim it so that it just touches the first fold
line. When this is pressed into place, reverse the
sail, mark the position and stick the second patch
down, matching its edge to the edge of the sail.
Then crease the sail and the patches along the
original fold lines and restitch the leech, taking care
that the leech-line is in position and undamaged.

If the tabling is of the kind that has been cut off
and resewn, first unpick it back far enough so that
you can patch the sail as above, then repair the
tabling taking care to get the tensioning correct.
The easiest way to do this is to stitch one end of the
repair strip onto the tabling first (after the main
patch is sewn into place), lay the tabling back into
position and mark the other end of the repair patch
onto the original cloth. Stick this in place and sew
it across twice. Trim off the frayed ends near the
tear, close to the inside row of stitching. Then sew
the tabling back to the sail, matching the stitching
holes. (See Figure 55)

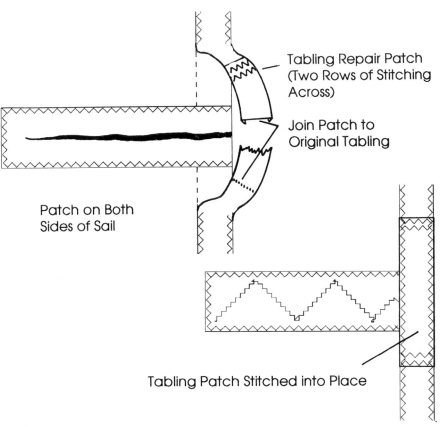

Tabling Repair Patch
(Two Rows of Stitching
Across)

Join Patch to
Original Tabling

Patch on Both
Sides of Sail

Tabling Patch Stitched into Place

Fig 55

Frayed Leech

6) The 'Instant Recut' should, for a proper repair, be
rebuilt as necessary. Unpick the emergency
stitching and press the sail flat with a warm iron. If
the cloth is badly frayed it should be renewed panel
by panel. (Rather than trying to sew on one huge
patch.)

For this you will need sailcloth to match the
weight and construction of your sail and you
should align it so that the warp (threads that run
along the length of the sailcloth) and weft (threads
that run across the sailcloth) are aligned.

Unpick the seams to 20cm back from the furthest-in damage on each frayed panel. Mark a pencil line at right-angles to the seam and halfway between the end of the unpicked stitching and the damaged cloth. (This is the line to which you will lay the replacement patch.) It is better to stagger the patches so that the joins on each panel do not meet at the same point on each seam.

Spread the sail out flat and lay a soft rope from the head down the part of the leech that is still solid, in a smooth curve to the clew. Mark inside the rope onto the ground with chalk; this will be the finished line for the new panel patches.

For each panel, cut the new sailcloth with a hot-knife or soldering iron at right-angles to the selvedge. With double-sided tape, stick the cut edge to the penciled line, matching the selvedges. (If the cloth you are using as patching is wider than the panels in your sail, you can either cut it down to match or overlap the extra bit for additional reinforcement. (See Figure 56)

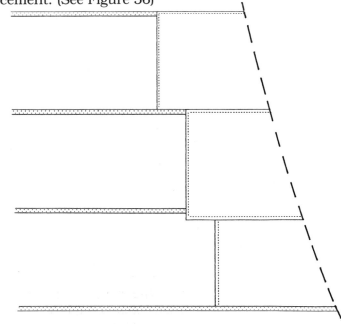

Fig 56

Photo 19. The finished permanent repair for a frayed leech.

Stitch the new cloth to the old, panel by panel, along the cut edge. Turn the inset pieces back and cut the old cloth away 5cm inside the join. Sew along this edge and repeat the process on each panel. Then,spreading the sail out so that there is equal tension on each panel, stick or pin them together and stitch along the seams.

With the sail spread out again, turn the leech over at the chalk line and crease it with a warm iron. If the sail leech is turned over (tabled) for a hem, make sure that the fold lines above and below the repair match up. If the leech is taped, cut the cloth at the fold line and stitch a double length of sail tape over the raw edge, reinforcing the stitching at each end.

Clew and Tack Repairs

7) Torn-out or Corroded Eye at Head, Tack or Clew.
   If you have repaired this strongly enough as
previously described (See Page 85), then there is
little more that can be done to improve it unless
you can find a heavy-duty sewing machine to stitch
around the edges of the webbing straps.

Damaged Reef Points

8) To repair a torn reef point it is best to remove the
original one together with the grommet, before
patching the side of the sail. For a repair that will
not look out of place, try to make the repair patch
the same shape as the reef point – for example, if it
was a diamond shaped patch, cut two repair
patches of the same shape and sufficiently large to
overlap the damaged area by at least 5cm all round.
Tack or stick these patches each side of the sail,
sew them in place with two rows of stitching all
round, than cut a new reef point patch the same
size as the original and stitch it in place. Make
additional stitching from corner to corner, side to
side and top to bottom of the repair patch through
the reef point patch. (See Figure 57)
   Then replace the grommet as close as possible to
its original position.

Broken Battens

9) These are the cause of seventy five percent of
repair work on mainsails and mizzens. The easiest
way to repair a torn pocket, at either the inner or
outer end, is with stick-on patches on both sides,
stitched down at each edge or around the bottom
(inner end). If this does not last, unpick the inner
end of the pocket and put a longer and wider patch
underneath on both sides of the sail before

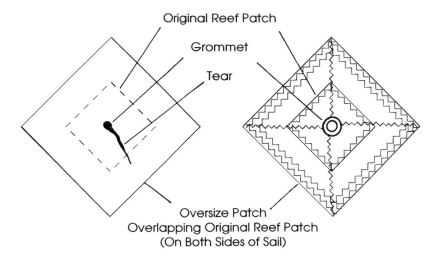

Original Reef Patch

Grommet

Tear

Oversize Patch
Overlapping Original Reef Patch
(On Both Sides of Sail)

Fig 57

stitching the pocket back in place. Then examine
the batten ends for sharp corners, the most likely
cause of the problem.

Battens do not have to be a really tight fit and it
is better for the sail if they are not forced into the
pocket. If they do not have plastic end-caps, a
length of masking tape or insulating tape wrapped
around the ends will stop them cutting into the
sailcloth.

Broken Slides

10) (See chapter 2, Page 61, Fig 35)
All that you can do is carry sufficient spare slides
and fastenings.

Mainsail Foot Repair

11) Foot slides or 'slugs'
Carry enough spares and the webbing or shackles
to fasten them.

12) Mainsail foot bolt rope.

If the sail starts to tear along the foot where the tape holding the bolt rope meets the sail, the only method of repair is to run a strip of sail tape the entire length of the foot. This is not an easy repair , as the rope will need to be stretched to its full extent from tack to clew and the tape attached with double-sided tape or contact glue while the tension on the rope is equal to that of the sail. If you can stretch the foot sufficiently so that the tape will lie flat and you are intending to stitch it by hand, do the sewing while it is pulled taught. If you have a sewing machine, wait till the contact glue is set before you release the tension. (Even so, it is worth tacking the tape in place before releasing the sail.)

The bolt rope will almost certainly show the first signs of wear at the tack where it emerges from the groove. Al that can be done here is to put on a patch of PVC, sail tape or iron-on cloth and endeavour to round off the entry point with a fine file. (Or consider tightening down the tack attachment.) The only other alternative is to use 'slug slides' the same diameter as the bolt rope, along the foot, which can be fastened with grommets as per the mast slides. These will make the sail a little fuller as the sail will be about 3cm above the boom. The best way to attach these is with webbing. (See Fig 35, page 61)

Chapter 6

Sewing Tips

Hand Stitching
When repairing a seam that has split some way into
the body of the sail, it will be easier to sew if the
seam is first stuck together. Either use double-
sided sticky tape or run a thin line of clear contact
glue down the centre between the old stitching
holes. This will help to maintain the correct cloth
tension. It is often easier to do this job with an
assistant. Drape the sail over the boom so that the
glued seam is parallel to the deck and halfway
between it and the boom. With a person on each
side, pass the needle back and forth through the
original stitch holes, pulling it out each side with a
pair of pliers.

If sewing is needed on a corner patch and
through several layers of cloth, it will help to punch
holes along the stitching line first, using a thin
spike and a rubber mallet. In this way there is less
chance of breaking the needle.

Machine Stitching
The major problem here is to pass the bulk of the
sail through the arm of the machine. To make this
easier, fold and roll the sail first, leaving the
damaged seam exposed. See Figure 58.

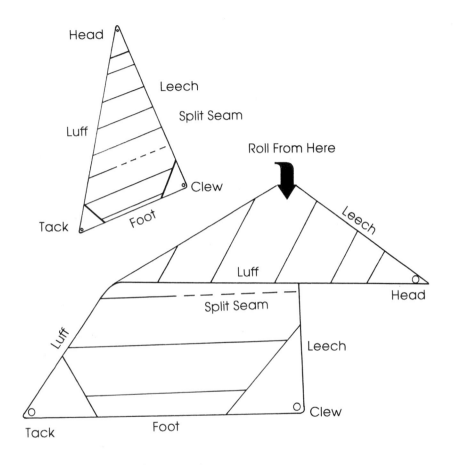

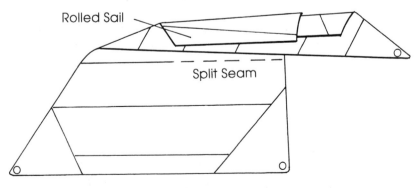

Fig 58

Chapter 7
Some Useful Sew-It-Yourself Ideas

A High-Visibility Water Catcher/Sun Awning

Many off-the-shelf 'Safety-Packs' contain a smallish square of orange cloth, usually plastic or PVC, with grommets at each corner and designed as a visibility aid in emergency situations. This is often not large enough to be seen from any distance and not made of material with the strength to hold up in bad weather conditions, when of course it is most likely to be required.

Since space is at a premium on most yachts, here is an idea for a multi purpose 'Instant Awning' – 'Visibility Aid' – 'Water Catcher', that can be folded and stowed in its own bag, takes up minimal space, will not rot or mildew and can easily be rigged for any of its uses.

Many sailmakers, tent makers or canvas shops will stock heavyweight orange PVC. For this design you will require a square, half the length of the main boom for each side, plus 8cm on each edge to allow for a strong doubled hem all round. If this means that you have to join two lengths together, ensure that they are stitched edge to edge first and then oversewn to flatten and strengthen the seam. (See Figure 59)

First Stitch Line
(Edge to Edge)

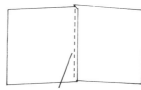

Second Stitch Line (Along Seam)
From Outside

Fig 59

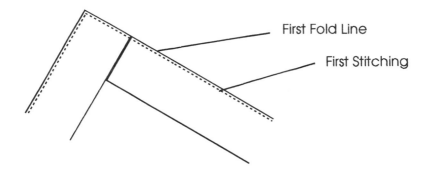

First Fold Line

First Stitching

Fig 60

Alternatively, you may find somewhere, such as a tent or awning manufacturer, with a heat-welding machine who can weld the seam for you. Even so, it is still worth running a line of zigzag stitching down the seam for added strength.

Draw a line 4cm in from the cut edge all round the outside of the cloth. Turn the edges over at this line and stitch along the crease. (See Figure 60)

Still on the outside, draw a line 4cm inside the first fold line. This is the turn-over line for the hem which will hold the reinforcing cord. This cord should be at least 3mm thick and braided line is preferable to laid-line because it stretches less. Cut the cord long enough to go round all sides, plus 10cm for the join. Knot one end so that it cannot slip inside and sew the cord in along the marked line (using a close-sewing or zipper foot), leaving 20cm open to allow you to join the cord ends together. (See Figure 61)

Finish the line of stitching with a zipper-foot as close as possible around the joined cord ends.

Then sew down the inner hem edge, folding the corners in and sewing along the folds. (See Figure 62)

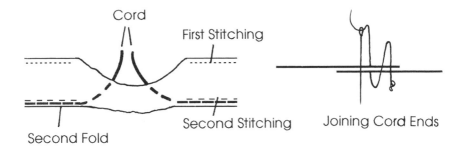

Cord
First Stitching
Second Stitching
Joining Cord Ends
Second Fold

Fig 61

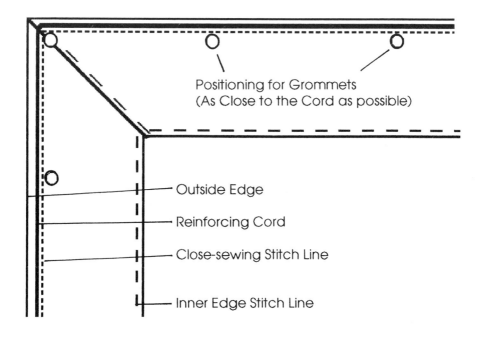

Positioning for Grommets
(As Close to the Cord as possible)

Outside Edge

Reinforcing Cord

Close-sewing Stitch Line

Inner Edge Stitch Line

Fig 62

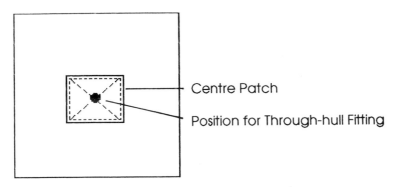

Centre Patch

Position for Through-hull Fitting

Fig 63

Lay the awning flat and draw a line from corner to corner. Where they intersect, punch a hole as a centre mark. Cut two pieces of the same cloth 30cm square. Match the centres of each to the centre of the awning and stick them back to back and then sew them on with two lines of stitching round the edges and a line from corner to corner. (See Figure 63)

Cut a hole in the centre just large enough for a small plastic through-hull fitting. Insert this and seal it with silicone. For the eyelets use proper sail grommets (brass or stainless steel). You may have to ask a sailmaker to insert these for you. You will need at least five on each side, though for added strength seven or nine would be better.

Since this is designed as an emergency aid, it is worth sticking (or sewing) on some reflective strips that are easily found in chandlers or bicycle shops. These have the added advantage of being radar reflective.

So – here you have this sheet of heavily reinforced orange PVC. For what?

In an emergency it could save your life. Rigged as a shade cover over the boom, it will not only keep you cooler, but the bright colour and reflective strips will make you easy to see from a distance. Tied upside down under the boom – forward to the shrouds and aft to the lifelines (or even between coconut palms on a deserted atoll), the water catchment in a quick shower and even from overnight condensation, could be a life-saver.

In a dire emergency you could even consider using it as a sea anchor or drogue, although you would probably have to cut it free since it would be difficult to retrieve. (See Seachute)

When this useful item is made, fold it as compactly as possible and make a bag for it, preferably in orange and with large lettering, and keep it somewhere handy and readily accessible. I hope that you will never use it in anger but having spent two and a half weeks stranded on a reef, I wish I'd thought of it before!

Seachute – A Simplified Sea Anchor

A sea anchor or drogue, is one of the emergency items that you hope never to use. Like the storm jib and trysail, it will probably be stowed in the most inaccessible locker to allow space for more frequently used gear. But – when you need it you will want to lay your hands on it fast and know that it is ready for instant use.

The older designs, with a wire or metal ring around the mouth of the drogue, take up more space and are generally harder to handle than the later 'parachute' models which are equally effective.

These 'parachute types can be as simple or as complicated as you choose to make them. Here is a design for a model that is quick and easy to make , stows in its own bag in less space than a large bath towel and can be attached to a warp and streamed in seconds.

The best material to use is heavy sailcloth (8 – 10oz) rather than canvas. Sailcloth will saturate almost as fast (to allow it to sink), dry more quickly, last longer and stow in a smaller space.

The size of the 'Seachute' will depend on the length of the boat. Since you start by cutting a circle, a rough guide to measuring the diameter is 10cm diameter per metre of hull length. When finished, this will be approximately the suggested Admiralty formula. For multihulls, double the diameter.

The simplest way to mark the circle onto the cloth is to use a piece of string, a pencil and a pushpin. Tie the string loosely at the lower end of the pencil and knot the string at the measurement of the radius (half the diameter).

Lay the cloth out flat on a wooden surface, with the pin at the centre and the string fully extended, draw your circle. Cut round this line, if possible with a hot-knife to seal the edge.

Fold the circle in half, then in quarters and crease the fold lines lightly with the blunt edge of your cutting shears so that the centre point and quarter lines show clearly.

Cut a small circle (approx 20cm diameter) of the same or stronger weight, but colour contrasting cloth, as a reinforcing patch. Match the centres and quarter lines and stitch it to the larger circle on the outer side.

Cut one quarter out from the complete circle, just inside the crease lines to leave 1cm on each side as a turn-over. (See Figure 64)

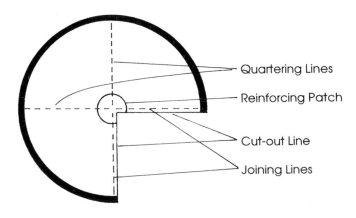

Quartering Lines

Reinforcing Patch

Cut-out Line

Joining Lines

Fig 64

Using a compass, mark a circle around the centre 10cm in diameter and another 1cm outside this. The first is the cutting line and the second is the sewing line for the webbing reinforcement.

This will form the 'spill-hole' at the narrow end, which is necessary to prevent the chute from oscillating when streamed.

Stitch round just inside the sewing line to hold the edges together and cut out the centre along the cutting line. (See Figure 65)

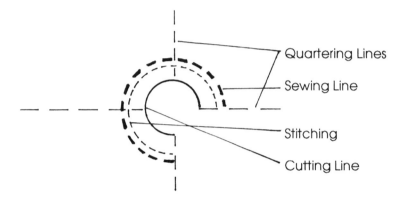

Quartering Lines

Sewing Line

Stitching

Cutting Line

Fig 65

Fold the 'Seachute' in half, with the right sides together, matching the cutting lines at the centre and outer edges. (See Figure 66)

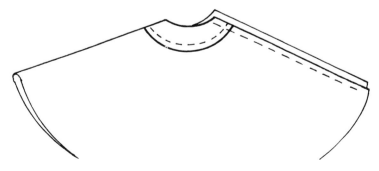

Fig 66

Straight-stitch along the sewing line and press the seams to one side. From the outside, zigzag stitch over the seam allowance to reinforce the seam and hold it in place. (See Figure 67)

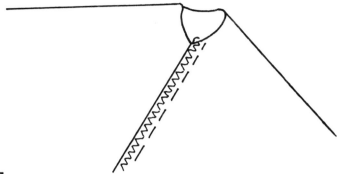

Fig 67

You will now need a short length of 2.5cm wide webbing, heat-sealed at both ends, to reinforce the narrow (aft) end. This will be easier to stitch on if the cloth is 'nicked' at 1cm intervals around the edge. (See Figure 68)

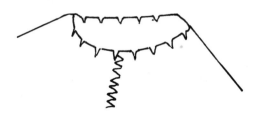

Fig 68

The webbing should be folded in half and stuck or tacked in place before stitching, with the ends overlapping by at least 1cm. Stitch it round with two rows of zigzag stitching, reinforcing the overlap. (See Figure 69)

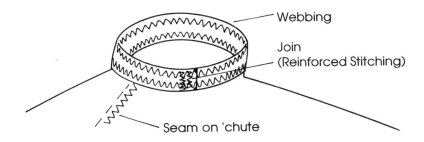

Fig 69

At the other end of the chute, mark a line 3cm in, all round. Take a length of 5cm wide webbing to match plus enough to allow for a 2cm overlap join at the ends. Stitch one side of the webbing to the line, reinforcing the overlap, then turn the other side over the chute edge and machine round it. (For accuracy and even stitching, tack it in place first.) Now sew round the outer edge. From the outside, you should have three rows of zigzag stitching showing on the webbing and two on the inside. (See Figure 70)

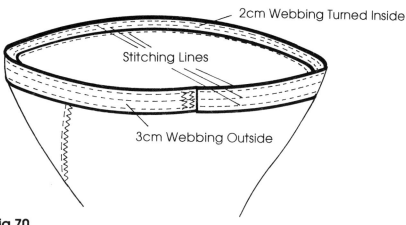

Fig 70

Fold the chute in half at the join. Mark the webbing at the opposite point and at one third intervals between these marks, giving six attachment points around the edge. At each mark insert a No 1 grommet between the outer and central stitching lines.

Measure the length of the seam on the chute, double it and add 20cm. Cut three lengths of 6mm braidline to this length and stitch them together at the centre.

Push the thimble over the swivel eye of a boat-snap, so that the wider upper end lies on the swivel eye. (See Figure 71)

Pass the three ends of the braidline through the swivel over the thimble, and matching the centre of the lines to the top of the thimble, stitch them together firmly in place at the lower end. (See Figure 72)

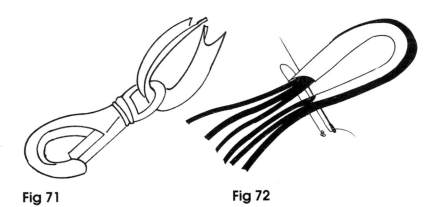

Fig 71   **Fig 72**

Fasten the snap-hook to a point high enough to allow the lines to dangle freely and making sure that they are all equal in length and not twisted at the top, tie each one to its appropriate grommet with a round turn and two half hitches, seizing the free end to the line above the knot. (See Figure 73)

The 'Seachute' has been extensively tested at sea. The one in the photograph was thrown over the stern of a Carter 33 which was sailing at six knots.

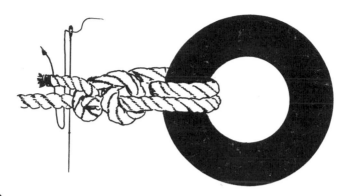

Fig 73

Within seconds the boat speed reduced to less than half a knot.

For recovery purposes, a trip line is not recommended as it could tangle around the drogue warp, fouling both warp and trip line. It is better to tie a small fender (coloured red) or an orange fishing float buoy, with 5m of 3mm line, to a grommet through the reinforcing patch at the narrow end of the chute and just inside the webbing. In this way, when the emergency is over and if you cannot pull in the chute, the warp can be released from the boat and picked up later with a boat hook. There is little chance of a float streamed like this tangling with the warp as it will stream aft of the chute and be pulled under by the load but surface when set free.

If you use a very heavy warp it may be sensible to add another fender at the boat end of the warp before cutting free.

'Seachute' Stow Bag

For the size, crease the chute lengthwise between the grommets and roll the excess cloth around it and over the lines. Measure the length and circumference. Cut a rectangle of cloth 5cm larger on two sides, fold it in half and machine along the length and lower edge. Turn the upper edge over

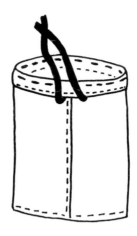

Fig 74

3cm and stitch the inner hem, leaving a 1cm gap either side of the seam to run a drawstring through. (See Figure 74)

Turn the bag right side out, knot the ends of the cord together and mark 'Seachute' on the outside.

Photo 20. 'Seachute' with recovery fender.

Emergency Fenders

If you are unlucky enough to be caught by a squall or surge whilst laying alongside a quay or jetty, there are times when even the most expensive 'blow-up' fender cannot stand the pressure. So – which would you rather lose, your boat or a cockpit cushion?

A folded-over cockpit cushion, with a length of rope through the crease, stuffed into a sail bag with the rope ends protruding and tied to the lifelines or to the jetty could save your hull. (Though neither the cushion or the bag will ever be the same afterwards!)

It is possible to make up 'Fender Pads' which can double as loose cockpit cushions, back-rests (if tied to the lifelines), sunbathing pillows – and still be handy if you do need emergency fenders.

Using old foam or discarded boat cushions, cut a rectangle twice the length of the width. Fold the cushion in half, run a rope through the fold and roughly stitch the two side edges together through the foam, catching the rope in the stitching at the upper corners. (See Figure 75)

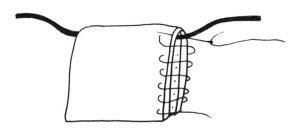

Fig 75

If you have any old canvas or sailcloth, it is better to cover these pads as they will then last longer and provide better protection for the hull.

Take a piece of cloth the width plus 2cm, and double the depth plus 4cm of the pad. Stitch down each side, leaving 2cm unsewn at the fold on each side. (See Figure 76)

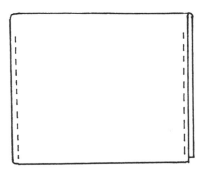

Fig 76

Turn the cloth the other way out, slip it over the pad and feed the ropes at the corners through the corresponding openings at the top corners of the cover. Loosely stitch the lower edges together.

Tie the pad to the jetty, not to the boat, thus ensuring that however much the boat moves, the hull is protected from damage.

Make Your Own Fenders

Fenders are an expensive necessity on any boat, especially in a marina, where your yacht is liable to damage – or be damaged by – your neighbours or the jetty if left unprotected. During winter storms, it is disheartening to see your expensive fenders becoming punctured and deflated, not to mention the damage caused to the hull. It is simple to make your own semi-solid fenders for little or no cost.

In most marinas, especially over the winter season, there will be boats renewing bunk or saloon cushions and throwing the old ones away. Here is a good source for the foam which you will require. Its condition is immaterial, but the thicker it is, the better. The ideal size is 2m or more long, 75 – 100cm wide and 8 – 15cm thick.

Saloon cushions are likely to be near enough rectangular, but if you find old shaped bunk cushions, wider at one end than the other, they are

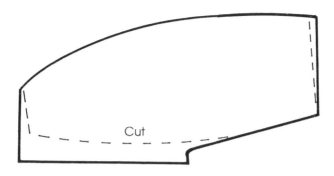

Fig 77

also ideal provided that you can trim off any angles and cut both sides roughly the same. (See Figure 77)

All you need is the foam, a length of line (an old mooring warp or sheet etc) five times the length of the widest part of the foam, a sheet of clear plastic about 80cm wider and longer than the cushion, insulating tape and some cheap material to make the cover.

Double the line and tie an overhand knot at the centre to form the eye. If the foam is a rectangle lay the line across the width at one end.
(See Figure 78)

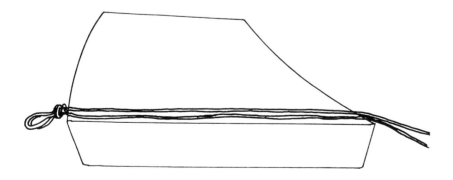

Fig 78

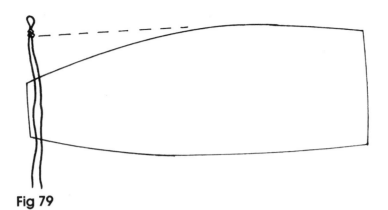

Fig 79

If you are using bunk cushion foam, lay the line on the narrowest end, with the knot level with the wider end. (See Figure 79)

Roll the foam tightly round the rope into a sausage shape and tape it round both ends and in the centre to hold it firmly. Take the free ends of rope, tie them together where they emerge from the roll, bring the ends up either side and pass them under the eye in the opposite direction.

See Figure 80.

Fig 80

Tie the two ends together with a reef knot and tuck the remaining rope back into the centre.

Lay the foam sausage onto one end of the plastic sheet, equidistant from each side and roll it up as tightly as possible, fastening it with tape just above and below the inner tape at both ends and around the centre.

At the top of the fender, gather the plastic together just below the knot and fasten it with waxed thread in a tight double clove-hitch to prevent rain soaking the foam.

At the bottom, fold it as if you were wrapping a bottle and add several turns of tape to keep it secure. Make a few holes in the plastic at the bottom . Although this means that the foam can absorb water, they will enable it to drain faster.

Directions for the fender cover follow.

Photo 21. The securing line, tied with a double overhand knot, positioned on an old bunk cushion at the start of the exercise.

Photo 22. The cushion has been tightly rolled and covered in its plastic film. Note that the rope tails have been brought back to the securing eye on the outside of the cushion, but inside the plastic.

Photo 23. Now resembling a fender, the bottom of the plastic covering remains to be secured before the fender cover is slipped over.

Fender Covers

To lengthen the life of your fenders and preserve the condition of your topsides, removable and washable fender covers are worth considering. These do not have to be made from expensive material as they will get damaged sooner or later. It is a lot cheaper to make another cover than to buy a new fender.

The covers need to be easy to remove and rinse out as they can trap salt, dust and grit which will abrade the hull.

Material to use.

Old sailcloth

Unless this is very lightweight or worn and supple (in which case it is likely to tear easily), it will be stiff and awkward to work with, especially when it comes to tensioning the drawstring at each end. Better keep spare sailcloth for patching the sails.

Canvas

If it is strong and heavy enough to last, it can present the same problems as sailcloth.

Acrylic

This is an expensive material – too good to use for this purpose and no better than cheaper alternatives.

Stretch towelling

Available from most general fabric stores and it is often possible to find 'roll-ends' or remnants for less than half-price.

Knitted stretch cotton jersey (T -shirt material)

This can sometimes be found in tubular form on rolls. This has the advantage that it can be stretched to fit any size of fender, but the disadvantage of being fairly thin and difficult to machine sew.

For standard shaped oblong fenders, measure from the top of the eye to the bottom of the fender and then around the circumference. Cut a rectangle of material this size plus 2cm on the circumference as a seam allowance. Stitch this side up, leaving a small gap at the top and bottom of the seam. (See Figure 81) Turn over a hem at the top and bottom edges with a drawstring emerging through the gap in the seam. Pull tight and thread it through the eye at each end or tie the ends together.

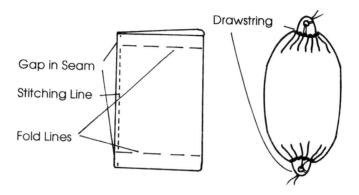

Drawstring

Gap in Seam

Stitching Line

Fold Lines

Fig 81

Photo 24. A self-made fender complete in its cover.

Photo 25. A fender cover on a typical off-the-shelf product.

Other ideas

If, like many cruising yachts, you are trying to save money and live on a tight budget and wish to protect your fenders, do not discard any of the following.

Worn-out jogging (or stretch) pants.
For small fenders, cut off below the knee, use the lower hem for one drawstring and turn over the upper edge for the top hem. For larger fenders use the thigh part of the pants, turning over top and bottom edges for the drawstring.

Cut-off Jeans
When the knees are worn through, and you turn them into shorts, save the legs. If your fenders are too fat to fit into the legs, split each leg down the inner seam and join them together (to fit the fender's circumference). Turn over the upper hem and cut off the lower edge to the right length, allowing for the turn-over.

Old T-shirts
If they have a design, turn them inside-out. Mark the stitching line on the outside, from the neck (which will take the upper drawstring).
   (See Figure 82)

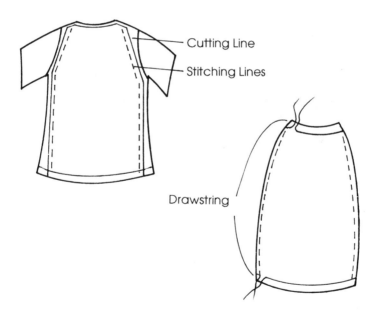

Turn the cover inside-out, so that the T-shirt pattern is on the inside. Use the drawstring at the 'neck' for the top end.

Fig 82

Index